Millionaire

Mentality

D0839704

Millionaire Mentality

As A Man Thinks, So Is He

Gary V. Whetstone

Gary Whetstone Publishing
New Castle, Delaware

What Christian Leaders Are Saying about the Ministry of Gary V. Whetstone

"...I have been in the pulpits of the world with Gary Whetstone, and...my personal witness of the anointing and the power that God uses through him literally changes lives. ...The quality and the depth of his teaching, its interdenominational flavor, its anointed power is something that I...encourage you to take advantage of. "

Charles Blair
Calvary Temple in Denver, CO

"...The level of teaching that [Pastor Gary Whetstone] brings to the table is absolutely incredible! You need this. It's going to take you to the next level.... When you get an opportunity to hear something that Pastor Whetstone has endorsed and prepared, you are dealing with somebody who's not just been in the boardroom, but has been right there on the field fighting...and he knows what he's talking about."

T.D. Jakes
The Potter's House

"Gary and Faye Whetstone attended our church in Tulsa before they began the powerful work that they now have in Delaware. We're excited for the new Bible training they have, to put God's Word practically into people's lives. They have a vision to reach the world for Jesus Christ.... We recommend highly what Gary and Faye Whetstone are doing in this new Bible Study training. Get plugged in!"

Billy Joe Daugherty
Victory Christian Center in Tulsa, OK

"...It's indeed a great honor...to talk to you about the incredible biblical study program under the anointed leadership of Gary Whetstone. First, I have known Gary for many, many years. Gary is an incredible pastor and teacher and evangelist to the nations of the world, and is spiritually qualified to head up this marvelous biblical study.... I wholeheartedly recommend this biblical study ministry under the leadership of Gary Whetstone...."

Morris Cerullo
World Evangelism, Inc.

"...I believe all those who sit under this anointed teaching...and the ministry of Pastor Whetstone at this remarkable school will be thoroughly equipped to gather in the end-time harvest before the imminent return of our Lord and Savior Jesus Christ."

Rod Parsley
World Harvest Church

Gary Whetstone Publishing
P.O. Box 10050
Wilmington, DE 19850 U.S.A.
Telephone: 1 (302) 324-5400
Fax: 1 (302) 324-5448
Web Site: www.gwwm.com
E-mail: info@gwwm.com

© 2000 by Gary V. Whetstone
All rights reserved. Published 2000
Printed in the United States of America
10 09 08 07 06 05 04 03 02 01 00   10 9 8 7 6 5 4 3 2 1

This book or parts thereof may not be reproduced in any form without prior written permission of the publisher. Italics have been added to some biblical verses for emphasis.

Unless otherwise indicated, all Scripture quotations are taken from the King James Version of *The Holy Bible.*

Scripture quotations marked (AMP) are taken from The Amplified Bible, Old Testament. Copyright © 1965, 1987 by The Zondervan Corporation. The Amplified New Testament, copyright © 1954, 1958, 1987 by The Lockman Foundation. Used by permission.

Scripture quotations marked (NIV) are taken from the HOLY BIBLE, NEW INTERNATIONAL VERSION®. NIV®. Copyright © 1973, 1978,1984 by International Bible Society. Used by permission of Zondervan Publishing House. All rights reserved.

Scripture quotations marked "NKJV" are taken from the New King James Version. Copyright © 1982 by Thomas Nelson, Inc. Used by permission. All rights reserved.

ISBN 1-928774-01-6 English
ISBN 1-928774-02-4 Spanish (Español)
ISBN 1-928774-07-5 French (Français)

For as he thinks
in his heart,
so is he....
Proverbs 23:7
(NKJV)

But thou shalt
remember the LORD thy God:
for it is he that giveth thee
power to get wealth,
that he may establish his covenant
which he sware unto thy fathers,
as it is this day.
Deuteronomy 8:18

Contents

Introduction

At the end of the week or month, do you have less money than you need? Regarding your financial situation, does it seem that your purse or wallet contains holes? Do you feel that you never have enough time to work *and* accomplish everything else you must do? Are you working so hard that you cannot enjoy your earnings? Do you dislike your job and wish you could find the perfect career? Does it weigh heavy on you to ponder the God-given dream in your heart, because you don't know how to accomplish it? Many people face stressful challenges such as these without knowing how to escape the frustration.

As a child, I often heard my father joke on payday that he was putting his paycheck into a "bag with holes." For ten years of my working life, I adopted my father's attitude and followed in his pathway regarding finances. Then, in 1978 I discovered biblical truths that set my finances free!

Now it is *your* turn. The Bible promises that God is no respecter of persons:

> Then Peter opened his mouth, and said, Of a truth I perceive that God is no respecter of persons.
> Acts 10:34

It is God's will for you to discover these biblical secrets. Then you can live in financial freedom, too. Ask yourself, *Am I following similar perspectives of lack? Am I ready for a breakthrough?* If so, this book is for you!

1

Proverbs 10:22 promises:

> The blessing of the LORD, it maketh rich, and he
> addeth no sorrow with it.
>
> Proverbs 10:22

Do you believe it is God's will to bless you? Do you realize His blessing produces wealth with no sorrow? Imagine your life if you experienced God's promise in Proverbs 10:22. Would you eliminate many activities that produce sorrow and financial frustration in your life? I believe your life will not be the same after you understand and implement God's principles concerning your wealth.

You see, God's Word contains all-powerful, never-changing principles designed to rule your circumstances. When you align yourself with His Word, these principles bless you perpetually and provide freedom in every area of life. In this book, we will study the progression of the biblical principles, which form what I call the *Millionaire Mentality*. These are **Purpose, Prophetic Vision, Pregnant Meditation, Proclamation, and Provision.**

As you read these pages, I pray that God will inspire you with clear answers about how to achieve His dreams in your heart. Get ready to embark on an exciting journey to personal fulfillment and biblical prosperity!

1
Birth the Millionaire Mentality

It took a Jewish lawyer for God to get my attention. Since then, my business and personal life have never been the same. The simple revelation I received from God one day revolutionized my perspective and birthed the *Millionaire Mentality.* I believe it will do the same for you!

In 1978, it all began when my wife, Faye, and I had begun a small business with only one thousand dollars and a desire for freedom from the everyday-working world. From our home, we had started selling wood stoves to several friends and coworkers. Because the U.S.A. was in the midst of an energy crisis, oil prices were so high that people were turning to alternative fuels to heat their homes. To our amazement, within two years we had owned five corporations with total gross sales of ten million dollars! With three retail stores, a thriving wholesale business, and a manufacturing-representative business, we were on the verge of launching our own franchise business.

At this point you might be thinking, *It's no wonder that you could think like a millionaire, because of all you had.* No, appearance is not necessarily reality, so don't jump to any conclusions yet!

You see, on most days, my wife and our staff worked tirelessly from 5:00 A.M. until 11:00 P.M. Soon, the businesses, which I had formed to bless my family, consumed us. The amount of work required was quickly becoming a huge burden. I found myself serving the very thing that I had created.

Something had to change, but I didn't know what. That's when God intervened in a very unexpected way—through a Jewish woman.

Who Planted the Garden of Eden?

During those years, I retained a tax lawyer to assist in decision making regarding our general business operations. She was a Jew, and I am a Christian. As you might expect, I continually witnessed to her about how to accept Jesus Christ and become saved. However, at one of our meetings, instead of my words changing her life, this Jewish lawyer made a statement that completely revolutionized *my* life!

I pray you will hear what I heard that day. In fact, I encourage you to take a moment to pray before you read any further. Ask God to give you ears to hear, in Jesus Name!

That day, when we had finished our business and I was about to leave my Jewish lawyer's office, she asked an unusual question. "Do you know why it is hard for some Jewish friends of mine to believe what you call the Gospel?"

My reply was very simple, "No."

The Jewish woman shared an insight into God's Word that I had never considered. Rising from her chair, she explained, "Let's go into the corporate record room. I want to show you something." On the far wall were shelves of the corporate books of her clients. She pointed to one thin book and said, "The owner is a Jew. He earns personally more than $500,000 annually as an absentee owner with very minimal work." Then one after another she shared the workload of many of her clients, all of whom are Jews. The last set of records was for my corporations. They were long and full. Instantly, I realized she knew something that I didn't.

Her next words pierced my heart. She asked, "Do you worry and constantly pray about finances? Do you have a life consumed with business to the point that you now live to serve your work? Are you fulfilled by the corporations you created, or are you spending too much time and money with little return?" At this point, I knew she had a very accurate picture of my life—maybe yours, too.

After returning to her office, we both sat as she looked straight into my eyes and asked, "Who planted the Garden of Eden?"

To my embarrassment, I really didn't know. Then, the Christians I attended church with only quoted from the New Testament. You see, they thought Jesus had fulfilled the Old Testament, and the promises God gave to the Israelites were not for today. Later, however, I discovered this is not true! All God's promises in the Old *and* New Testaments are ours.

Well, my lawyer reached into her drawer and pulled out the Pentateuch—the first five books in the Bible. As she read the Scriptures to me, I felt like *she* was converting *me!* "A Jew converting a Christian?" you might ask. Yes. That day, my Jewish lawyer taught me important truths from the Old Testament that I had not known before.

She began to read from the first book:

> And *the LORD God planted a garden eastward in Eden;* and there he put the man whom he had formed.
>
> And *out of the ground made the LORD God to grow every tree* that is pleasant to the sight, and good for food; the tree of life also in the midst of the garden, and the tree of knowledge of good and evil.
>
> And *a river went out of Eden to water the garden;* and from thence it was parted, and became into four heads.
>
> The name of the first is Pison: that is it which

compasseth the whole land of Havilah, where *there is gold;*
   And *the gold of that land is good: there is bdellium and the*
onyx stone.
   And the name of the second river is Gihon: the same
is it that compasseth the whole land of Ethiopia.
   And the name of the third river is Hiddekel: that is it
which goeth toward the east of Assyria. And the fourth
river is Euphrates.
   And *the LORD God took the man, and put him into the*
garden of Eden to dress it and to keep it.

Genesis 2:8-15

Here was the answer to my lawyer's question: "Who planted
the Garden of Eden?" God Himself had planted it, and through
it He lavished man with provisions and prosperity!

Listening intently to every word, I experienced a new insight
into God's plan for man. As my lawyer read the Word of God,
I thought, *Wow! In the Old Covenant, God revealed wisdom to the*
Jews to release them from financial bondage. Now, I want those
promises to work in my life, too.

Then, this Scripture immediately came to my mind:

   He that walketh with wise men shall be wise: but a
   companion of fools shall be destroyed.

Proverbs 13:20

I was ready for a change in my life to avoid destruction. I
decided right then that I would heed this wisdom.

My lawyer continued to explain that for every man God has
planted a garden designed to serve that man. The revelation
struck my heart: *I have a field that God planted for me.* He planted
it, watered it, and made it grow for me. In my field is all the
provision I need—like gold, bdellium, and onyx stones were in

Eden for Adam and Eve. In fact, God created the earth to work for man, not man to work for the earth! Suddenly, my eyes began to open. I realized that my job in my God-given garden is simply to harvest it!

You see, Adam's sin brought the curse of man working for the earth. This was not God's original intention. Adam's disobedience opened the door for this curse:

> And unto Adam he [God] said, Because thou hast hearkened unto the voice of thy wife, and hast eaten of the tree, of which I commanded thee, saying, Thou shalt not eat of it: cursed is the ground for thy sake; in sorrow shalt thou eat of it all the days of thy life;
>
> Thorns also and thistles shall it bring forth to thee; and thou shalt eat the herb of the field;
>
> In the sweat of thy face shalt thou eat bread, till thou return unto the ground; for out of it wast thou taken: for dust thou art, and unto dust shalt thou return.
>
> Genesis 3:17-19

Suddenly, Adam's field began to produce thorns and thistles. Now, he had to work for the land instead of it working for him.

My Jewish lawyer continued to share that many Christians tie themselves to the curse because they think that making a profit or being wealthy is sinful. Finally, we ended our conversation with a little humor. I concluded, "Well, I guess that's why the cliché isn't 'as poor as a *synagogue*-mouse'!" No, the accepted norm for many people today is "as poor as a *church*-mouse."

God, What Is My Field?

The following week, I flew to the state of Washington.

7

There, I met with a manufacturer from whom my company bought about $750,000 (U.S. dollars) of products annually. At approximately 5:00 A.M., I awoke and began asking God to show me the field He had planted for me.

Instantly, the Holy Spirit spoke to my spirit, directing me to resign as a distributor of their materials. He instructed me explicitly. I was to offer to represent this manufacturer's products to distributors east of the Mississippi River at a commission rate of 12%.

I met with the manufacturer over breakfast and shared about finding the field God had planted for me. After I released our distributorship, the company, in turn, contracted with me to represent their products. Hallelujah, it had worked! The financial pressure left. I did not need to borrow any more money for inventory. Suddenly, my warehouse, trucks, employees, all the overhead expenses, and the associated pressures were unnecessary.

As a result of that one thought from God, I received my first commission check for $50,000 within one month! The amount of work was less than one week, and my costs were under $1,000! I had found my field. It was working for *me*. No longer did I need to slave over it to get results. This event forever changed how I *perceive* God, which determines how I *receive* from God now.

Let me encourage you that God has planted a field for *you*, too. In a later chapter, I will outline a practical plan to help you find your God-ordained field. Through your field, He will provide everything you need to accomplish His will for your life and achieve a sense of fulfillment. However, before you find your field and start letting it work for you, you must understand a very important principle. I must caution you that the next chapter is critical to your success and fulfillment. Be sure to read it carefully.

2
What Is the Purpose of Your Wealth?

Many people subconsciously believe that striving for riches is wrong, yet they spend most of their waking hours laboring for paychecks. Others believe that acquiring money and wealth will bring satisfaction. However, the peace and joy of knowing we are in God's will gives His children true fulfillment.

In this chapter, we will discuss God's will regarding your prosperity, how to avoid the snare of accumulating wealth for the wrong reasons, and why this knowledge is critical to your success. Now, let's examine the first of five principles that lead to a *Millionaire Mentality:* Purpose.

Know Its Purpose Before You Get It

First, you must know the purpose of something before you can adequately understand its provision or how to obtain it. In other words, knowing why you do something enables you to know *what* to do and *how*. Without answering the "why" of purpose, you cannot have the "what" of provision. You see, if a person does not know why something exists, he is very likely to use it for the wrong purpose. This ultimately can turn into abuse, causing the person to lose the very thing he sought.

This is true with riches. Many people do not understand the purpose of wealth. They yield to the temptation of accumulating money for purposes other than God's original intention. At times, even Christians can do this. Many face financial conflicts without recognizing God's will. Some continually struggle with their finances and cannot free their minds of the pressure. This stress often leads to family breakups, health challenges, and difficulties in every arena. It breaks my heart to see this many people in financial bondage when God already has provided the answers.

Well, what *is* the purpose of wealth, and why does God want you to have it? Deuteronomy 8:18 declares:

> But thou shalt remember the LORD thy God: for it is he that giveth thee power to get wealth, *that he may establish his covenant* which he sware unto thy fathers, as it is this day.
>
> Deuteronomy 8:18

God's original purpose of wealth was to establish His covenant on earth. In the book of Genesis, the Bible explains God's covenant with Abraham (previously named Abram) for the Jews. Although we will discuss this further in later chapters, notice God's promise in the following verses:

> In the same day the LORD made a covenant with Abram, saying, Unto thy seed have I given this land....
>
> And I will make of thee a great nation, and I will bless thee, and make thy name great; and thou shalt be a blessing:
>
> And I will make my covenant between me and thee, and will *multiply thee exceedingly.*
>
> As for me, behold, my covenant is with thee, and thou shalt be a father of many nations.
>
> Genesis 15:18; 12:2; 17:2, 4

Ever since this covenant, the world has never considered the Jews to be a poor people.

Earlier I mentioned the idiom, "as poor as a church-mouse." It is not "as poor as a synagogue-mouse." Why? Isn't it true that, through Jesus Christ, Christians have a better covenant than the Jews, which God established upon better promises? What changed the Church's mindset to believe that we are as poor as church mice? Many accept the attitude that the Church does not have enough financially, and therefore even the rodents living in the church house lack. The leftovers from a Christian's life is not enough to keep even a mouse alive.

Christians who believe this are grieving the Holy Spirit. The truth is God not only has great plans for His people, but He also provides the means to accomplish them. Yet, we struggle in lack and take His dreams to our graves. It breaks God's heart.

You see, the work of Christ at Calvary engrafted His believers into God's covenant with Abraham. Now, we can live in limitless relationship with God. In fact, we have an exceedingly better covenant than Abraham, because we have Christ dwelling in us through the Holy Spirit. If you are a Christian, this is true for you, too.

God's Covenant with You

To better understand God's covenant with His people and His purpose for wealth, let's study the eighth chapter of Deuteronomy. What was God's plan when the children of Israel wandered in the wilderness for 40 years? How does this affect you?

In verse one, at God's prompting, Moses explained to the Israelites:

> All the commandments which I command thee this day shall ye observe to do, *that ye may live, and multiply, and go in and possess the land* which the LORD sware unto your fathers.
>
> Deuteronomy 8:1

Here, we see that God gave the commandments so the Israelites would experience a moral, disciplined lifestyle. Obeying these would qualify them for His promises. Many times, we see the Law of Moses simply as a way to reveal man's sin and to control moral behavior. However, the original purpose of the commandments was to enable the Israelites to obtain God's desired blessings for them. We must understand that God did not intend Israel to lack but instead to walk in His promises. Then, we can appreciate the commandments in a new way.

Moses continued:

> And thou shalt remember all the way which the LORD thy God led thee these forty years in the wilderness, *to humble thee, and to prove thee, to know what was in thine heart, whether thou wouldest keep his commandments, or no.*
>
> Deuteronomy 8:2

It is difficult to know a person's true character until he faces stress. Pressure reveals the hidden nature. In the above verse, we learn that God decided to test Israel to see if they would obey Him. So He led them into a 40-year "pressure cooker." God also knew that He could determine if they were wise by correcting them, because a wise person benefits from correction and reproof. Yet, a fool turns against authority.

> A reproof entereth more into a wise man than an

hundred stripes into a fool.

Proverbs 17:10

A fool despiseth his father's instruction: but he that regardeth reproof is prudent.

Proverbs 15:5

Now, God walked throughout the trial with the Israelites:

And he humbled thee, and suffered thee to hunger, and fed thee with manna, which thou knewest not, neither did thy fathers know; that he might make thee know that *man doth not live by bread only, but by every word that proceedeth out of the mouth of the LORD doth man live.*

Deuteronomy 8:3

God wanted the nation of Israel to live on the sustaining revelation of His Word, not on the provision they could earn with their own hands. Thus, His desire was that they become *revelation oriented,* not *provision oriented.*

God proved the Israelites for 40 years, so they would learn that man does not live by bread alone but by every Word from God. You see, provision comes from God's voice. However, the Israelites chose not to expect their supply from their Heavenly Father's voice. In fact, they did not even want to hear from Him. Think of it: The Israelites spent 40 years in the wilderness, because they would not hear and obey God. Thus, they could not walk in His promises!

Now, because of the finished work of Jesus Christ, the Church has far better promises than Israel ever had. Yes, God tested the Israelites for a season to prove whether they would obey Him *before* He released the provision. Today, there must be a reason some Christians do not have the release of God's provision. Perhaps it is because they have not yet proven they will hear and obey God and be willing to live by His every Word. (We will discuss more about this later in this chapter.) God's nature does not change. The way the Lord communicated and tested in the Old Testament is the same as today.

> Jesus Christ the same yesterday...to day, and for ever.
> Hebrews 13:8

God forged Israel to become an obedient people in an unfriendly land. Jesus also learned obedience through His suffering in a hostile environment. Similarly, during its days of persecution, God formed the early Church to obey Him in an antagonistic setting. It is highly likely that we face a hostile atmosphere to motivate us to obey God's Word, too. If Jesus had to learn obedience through suffering, it is certain that we will not escape the same.

You may be thinking, *I thought this book was about Millionaire Mentality—how to get money.* It is, but you need to do it according to God's plan, not the flesh's way. There is a big difference. You can get money by robbing or in legal ways but for the wrong reasons. However, these ungodly methods and motivations will not produce blessings in your life. You see, I am not writing simply about money, but about its connection with God's purpose. This is about what He desires to form within you, so you will be trustworthy with whatever He puts into your hands. Otherwise, any wealth you accumulate will be a curse to you.

Now, when you begin to accumulate wealth and blessings God's way, it is critical that you remember where it came from:

> For the LORD thy God bringeth thee into a good

land, a land of brooks of water, of fountains and depths that spring out of valleys and hills;

A land of wheat, and barley, and vines, and fig trees, and pomegranates; a land of oil olive, and honey;

A land wherein thou shalt eat bread without scarceness, thou shalt not lack any thing in it; a land whose stones are iron, and out of whose hills thou mayest dig brass.

When thou hast eaten and art full, then thou shalt bless the LORD thy God for the good land which he hath given thee.

Beware that thou forget not the LORD thy God, in not keeping his commandments, and his judgments, and his statutes, which I command thee this day:

Lest when thou hast eaten and art full, and hast built goodly houses, and dwelt therein;

And when thy herds and thy flocks multiply, and thy silver and thy gold is multiplied, and all that thou hast is multiplied;

Then thine heart be lifted up, and thou forget the LORD thy God, which brought thee forth out of the land of Egypt, from the house of bondage;

Who led thee through that great and terrible wilderness, wherein were fiery serpents, and scorpions, and drought, where there was no water; who brought thee forth water out of the rock of flint;

Who fed thee in the wilderness with manna, which thy fathers knew not, that he might humble thee, and that he might prove thee, to do thee good at thy latter end;

And thou say in thine heart, My power and the might of mine hand hath gotten me this wealth.

Deuteronomy 8:7-17

Remember, God tested the children of Israel so He could bless them in the end. However, when the blessings came, God did not want the Israelites to become slack in trusting and obeying Him.

I have watched many people cross the threshold into prosperity. Beforehand, they had correctly tithed and given offerings. Their declarations, actions, and motivations had been consistent with God's Word. Then, creative ideas had started to flow. Financial increase had come, and the power of God's anointing had infiltrated their hearts and lives. However, at that point, they began to think the fruit of their cultivation and development was enough to sustain them. Suddenly, they forgot God. Then, many kinds of difficulties and negative situations happened to them. I have found it better to prove to God that we will trust and obey Him *before* we obtain His blessings. Otherwise, the blessings may become our downfalls.

Let's read the *next* two verses after Deuteronomy 8:18:

> But thou shalt remember the LORD thy God: for it is he that giveth thee power to get wealth, that he may establish his covenant which he sware unto thy fathers, as it is this day.
>
> And it shall be, if thou do at all forget the LORD thy God, and walk after other gods, and serve them, and worship them, I testify against you this day that ye shall surely perish.
>
> As the nations which the LORD destroyeth before your face, so shall ye perish; because ye would not be obedient unto the voice of the LORD your God.
>
> Deuteronomy 8:18-20

God wants you to be in the flow of money. However, if you forget Him and His purpose for wealth, then you can lose it as quickly as you obtained it.

We have learned from Deuteronomy that God would not give the Promised Land to the nation of Israel until He had an obedient people. Today, when I find a group of people not walking in the provision of God's vision, I realize there is a reason for it. This may sound harsh, but the truth is they may not yet be trustworthy. They may not have passed the test of obedience in some area of their lives. Now, these people may have good intentions, but you know the adage: "The road to Hell is paved with good intentions." Good intentions do not merit God's blessings. To obtain prosperous results, you must fellowship with God and obey Him.

Let's read the Amplified version of a passage in Isaiah:

> Thus says the Lord, your Redeemer, the Holy One of Israel: I am the Lord your God who teaches you to profit, Who leads you by the way that you should go.
>
> Oh, that you had hearkened to My commandments! Then your peace and prosperity would have been like a flowing river; and your righteousness [the holiness and purity of the nation] like the abundant waves of the sea;
>
> Your offspring would have been as the sand, and your descendants like the offspring of the sea; their name would not be cut off or destroyed from before me.
> Isaiah 48:17-19 (AMP)

In effect, God said to the Israelites here, "If only you had listened to and followed Me, You would have experienced a constant flow of prosperity in your lives. Instead, look at what you reaped. I would have perpetuated blessings through your children. However, now it must cease." Israel then returned to bondage.

God's design is to teach you to excel, prosper, and profit with waves of prosperity crashing in your life. Therefore, should a still pond satisfy you? No, believe and expect Him to release torrents of blessing and prosperity in your direction!

Do you realize that more money exists on this earth than people know what to do with? Yet, how many of us think we don't have enough? The problem is our perspective. It's time to change our thinking about money. We will discuss more about this in a later chapter.

Follow God's Plan of Wealth

One day, God spoke to me, saying it was my time for supernatural increase. Then, I had an opportunity to buy stock, which was selling at or about 30 cents per share. However, fear gripped me, and I did not buy it. Within a matter of days, the closing price on this stock was $2.90 per share! Now, believe me, I am not advocating buying stock. However, I now realize that because I did not listen to God's voice, I lost my opportunity to profit.

How can you reclaim lost opportunity? You cannot. The generations of Israelites who died in the wilderness did not receive their portions of God's promises. It is simple: When you do not follow the Lord's directions, you lose His blessings. This is heart wrenching, but God does not guarantee unconditional *blessings.* He only guarantees unconditional *love.* In other words, God will love you regardless of whether or not you choose to serve Him and receive blessings!

Some might say, "But He's the God of a second chance." This is a nice statement but not a guarantee. When I read my Bible, I see that many people did not receive second chances. In fact, some disobeyed and died the next day! Not everyone automatically has a second, third, or fourth chance with God.

When this does happen, we should thank Him for His Grace, but not plan our lives around it. It is far better to obey God when He speaks than to continue failing Him repeatedly like Israel did. Following God's purpose the first time is how you pass His tests.

Analyze this. Ask yourself, *Am I in a time of testing to prove if I will live by every Word that proceeds from the mouth of God? Do I believe that my sustenance will come through God's promises, if I am obedient to Him? Does He count me trustworthy of what He will put into my hands?* These are critical issues to resolve. It does not matter whether you are a new babe in Christ, a very mature Bible-quoting believer, somewhere between these, or not a Christian at all. God wants to see if He can trust you.

The Bible promises:

> And all these blessings shall come on thee, and overtake thee, if thou shalt hearken unto the voice of the LORD thy God.
>
> Deuteronomy 28:2

Deception can cause anyone to think he is right with God. However, if God's blessings are not overtaking you, something is wrong. I have heard it said, "God will never advance you…beyond your last act of disobedience." Do you feel stuck in a life of lack or not feel fulfilled? Be honest with yourself as you check your heart. Ask the Lord to reveal any areas of disobedience in your life or arenas in which you do not *completely* trust Him.

God Desires to Prosper His People

God's idea has never been for His people to lack. Throughout His Word, we find the opposite is true.

> O taste and see that the LORD is good: blessed is the

man that trusteth in him.

O fear the LORD, ye his saints: for there is no want to them that fear him.

The young lions do lack, and suffer hunger: but they that seek the LORD shall not want any good thing.

Psalm 34:8-10

Let them shout for joy, and be glad, that favour my righteous cause: yea, let them say continually, Let the LORD be magnified, which hath pleasure in the prosperity of his servant.

Psalm 35:27

Here, the Bible says to magnify the Lord, who takes pleasure in my prosperity. I would much rather make God happy by blessing and prospering me than upset Him by being needy and wanting! What about you?

Remember, Proverbs 10:22 says:

The blessing of the LORD, it maketh rich, and he addeth no sorrow with it.

Proverbs 10:22

Do you wake up every morning, shouting for joy because of God's provision, or do you speak from a sorrowful motivation? "I can't imagine where the money will come from. Another day, another dollar. It's murky Monday, tribulation Tuesday, what's-it-all-worth Wednesday, thankless Thursday, or frazzled Friday. It will be a miracle, if I get through the week. That miserable paycheck I get is never enough money to do anything with. Everyone wants to get hold of it: The government, my family, and even God. Everybody has a hand in my pocket."

Do you feel that the money you earn each week is not

fulfilling your dreams for tomorrow? Instead, have you already spent it the previous month and now must pay the bills? Working to pay off yesterday's expenses is not an exciting motivation to work with. Don't defeat yourself. Let God's Word revive your spirit. Here's what He has to say about your situation:

For the LORD God is a sun and shield: the LORD will give grace and glory: no good thing will he withhold from them that walk uprightly.

Psalm 84:11

For evildoers shall be cut off: but those that wait upon the LORD, they shall inherit the earth.

A little that a righteous man hath is better than the riches of many wicked.

I have been young, and now am old; yet have I not seen the righteous forsaken, nor his seed begging bread.

Psalm 37:9, 16, 25

Praise ye the LORD. Blessed is the man that feareth the LORD, that delighteth greatly in his commandments.

His seed shall be mighty upon earth: the generation of the upright shall be blessed.

Wealth and riches shall be in his house: and his righteousness endureth for ever.

Psalm 112:1-3

Honour the LORD with thy substance, and with the firstfruits of all thine increase:

So shall thy barns be filled with plenty, and thy presses shall burst out with new wine.

Proverbs 3:9-10

> Humility and the fear of the LORD bring wealth and honor and life.
>
> Proverbs 22:4 (NIV)

> If you are willing and obedient, you will eat the best from the land.
>
> Isaiah 1:19 (NIV)

> They will rebuild the ancient ruins and restore the places long devastated; they will renew the ruined cities that have been devastated for generations.
>
> Aliens will shepherd your flocks; foreigners will work your fields and vineyards.
>
> And you will be called priests of the LORD, you will be named ministers of our God. You will feed on the wealth of nations, and in their riches you will boast.
>
> Isaiah 61:4-6 (NIV)

These Scriptures are only a small sampling of biblical evidence that God desires to bless you financially. Read all 66 books of the Bible, and note every area that deals with finances, including work, income, wealth, riches, deceitfulness of riches, ownership, stewardship, and other related topics. If you do this, you will find more on this subject than any other topic in the entire Word of God. Do you know why? It is because your finances can influence you as much as God does.

Jesus said:

> No one can serve two masters. Either he will hate the one and love the other, or he will be devoted to the one and despise the other. You cannot serve both God and Money.
>
> Matthew 6:24 (NIV)

God knows how man thinks. People will invest 40 to 60 hours a week to earn money, yet complain about their pastor's Sunday message if it lasts more than 45 minutes. Here is an interesting thought: What would happen if we reversed the cycle? Why not spend 40 hours a week in the Word and one hour to get all the money we need? God took 40 years with Israel in the wilderness so they would learn that man does not live by bread alone but by every Word that proceeds from the mouth of God. However, man's mentality is we have to work for a living. Therefore, we spend only a little time with God, that is, if we take time at all to hear from Him.

Deuteronomy 28, which we will discuss in detail later, is a chapter of blessings and curses. The choice is ours regarding whom we will serve. Will we live in cursed or blessed environments? I made my own choice early. I decided it was worth spending more time in the Word than in trying to make money. Not surprisingly, I discovered there is more money in the Word than in making money! How do I get it? It comes from what God says to me. As I read and meditate on the Bible and spend time with God, He gives creative ideas to me that generate more income than when I "beat the bushes" in business on my own.

Listening to the voice of the Lord will release you from the stress of continually thinking about money and how to get or keep it. God will pour so many inspired ideas and blessings into you that you will not be able to contain them all. In His Word, He declares to you:

> I love those who love me,
> And those who seek me diligently will find me.
> Riches and honor are with me,
> Enduring riches and righteousness.

My fruit is better than gold, yes, than fine gold,
And my revenue than choice silver.
I traverse the way of righteousness,
In the midst of the paths of justice,
That I may cause those who love me to inherit wealth,
That I may fill their treasuries.

Proverbs 8:17-22 (NKJV)

Does this mean that God has no interest in money? No. Remember, He owns it all. He simply desires for you to use it properly. Think about it: God loves those who love Him and seek Him. He causes them to inherit wealth and have full treasuries!

While this book is about *Millionaire Mentality,* it does not necessarily mean that your balance sheet will show a net worth of millions of dollars. Actually, your mindset first should be that your worth is far greater than *any* amount of money.

You see, only when you comprehend the exorbitant price God paid for you, can you fully appreciate your dignity and personal value to Him. We know that the price someone is willing to pay for an item determines its true value. Your value to God is set. He already determined it by His awesome sacrifice of His only begotten Son!

Never underestimate what God wants to do with your life. Recognize that His Word declares:

Beloved, I wish above all things that thou mayest prosper and be in health, even as thy soul prospereth.

3 John 1:2

Now unto him that is able to do exceeding abundantly above all that we ask or think, according to the power that worketh in us.

Ephesians 3:20

I pray that God will open the eyes of your understanding and cause you to see the entire financial and material arena from His viewpoint. Remember, how you perceive God is how you will receive from God! In the next chapter, we will discuss this further.

Let's close this chapter on the Purpose of wealth with a prayer:

Heavenly Father, thank You for establishing a holy covenant with me through Your Son, Jesus. I believe that, according to Your Word, You desire to bless and prosper me, and will cause me to fulfill Your heavenly dream for my life.

When Your blessings come upon me, Oh, Lord, help me not to forget You. Let me keep my eyes focused on You, Father, and not on wealth and prosperity. Help me to be a good steward of Your blessings. In Jesus' Name. Amen.

3
Find the Field God Planted for You

Never forget that how you perceive God will determine how you receive from God. You are very important to Your Heavenly Father. He has a vision for His Kingdom, and you have a vital role in His dream. To help you achieve it, He has prepared a place of provision. Locating it will free your time, so you can devote more effort and finances to His work instead of spending all your time working to earn a living. The key is finding that field. In this chapter, I will show you how to do that. Then, you will be well on your way to the second of five principles that lead to a *Millionaire Mentality:* Prophetic Vision.

Just One Word from God...

In 1983, my wife and I sold our businesses, then in 1984 began a church in our home with only three people. After a few months, I asked God why He had taken the gift of giving away from me. For many years before this, God had blessed us so we could substantially support His Kingdom's work both in the U.S.A. and abroad. Now, our income had significantly dropped.

The instant the words fell from my mouth, the Holy Spirit spoke to my spirit. "I have not taken the gift of giving from you," He said. "You have taken it from Me!"

I walked outside and asked, "Lord, where is the field You planted for me now?"

Immediately the Spirit of the Lord spoke to me again. This

time, He told me to buy my neighbors' house for $30,000. I realized that its market value was at least $75,000 then. However, I obediently walked to my neighbors' home and shared the revelation about God's field with the owners.

They immediately replied that the house was worth at least $75,000 and was not for sale!

After a little discussion, I left, saying, "When you are ready to sell it to me, just call."

Within three months, I received that call, and my neighbors sold their home to me for only $30,000. After a $10,000 cosmetic facelift, I sold the house in the same year for $97,000. Just one thought from God produced $57,000 gross profit.

I now maintain a perspective that God always has a field planted for me, which is ready to harvest. All I must do is learn from Him where it is and go reap the field.

Harvest the Field of Your Dreams

I believe the following verses apply to any field that God has planted for His children, whether it is preaching the Gospel to unbelievers, ministering, teaching, working in business, or any other work.

Jesus saith unto them, My meat is to do the will of him that sent me, and to finish his work.

Say not ye, There are yet four months, and then cometh harvest? behold, I say unto you, *Lift up your eyes, and look on the fields; for they are white already to harvest.*

And he that reapeth receiveth wages, and gathereth fruit unto life eternal: that both he that soweth and he that reapeth may rejoice together.

And herein is that saying true, One soweth, and another reapeth.

I sent you to reap that whereon ye bestowed no labour: other men laboured, and ye are entered into their labours.

John 4:34-38

As we continue our journey deeper into the *Millionaire Mentality*, get ready to see *your* field white and ready for harvesting before your eyes.

Now, I encourage you to examine your life carefully as we discuss the following important topics about you personally:

- What is a cursed field?
- Does my attitude directly affect my financial future?
- Where is my field that God planted for me?

For a very thorough and informative teaching about finding the specific field God planted for you, please refer to my eight-tape series (audio, video, or CD), *True Success—How to Find the Field God Has Planted for You*. Subjects include understanding the symptoms of a cursed field, how to escape the field of curse, identifying the origins of your work environment, recognizing your giftings versus your adaptations based upon financial need, coming out of need into God's purposes, and much more.

Biblical Identifications of a Cursed Field

Maybe you have a vision, but for years something has held you back, preventing you from marching toward its fulfillment. If you have felt a strangling or stifling of your dream, perhaps an unaware area of curse is in your life. Before proceeding, you must close all the open doors for curses to come. For practical strategies regarding breaking curses, please refer to my book and tape series *How to Identify and Remove Curses!*

To discover more about how the Fall in the Garden of Eden produced a curse on mankind, how to break free, and how to help set others free in Jesus' Name, consult my book *Conquering Your Unseen Enemies.*

Answering the following questions will help you to determine if you are in a cursed field. Be brutally honest with yourself as you read this section:

1. In your current employment, can you set your own income level and the direction of your vocation; or do you work for someone else, who determines what you are worth?

2. Do you thoroughly enjoy what you do, or is it only a means to get money? Your curse could be your motivation. We will discuss this further in the next section.

3. Is the work of your hands like the curse God gave to Adam, as we read earlier?

    ...Cursed is the ground for thy sake; in sorrow shalt thou eat of it all the days of thy life;
    Thorns also and thistles shall it bring forth to thee; and thou shalt eat the herb of the field;
    In the sweat of thy face shalt thou eat bread, till thou return unto the ground; for out of it wast thou taken: for dust thou art, and unto dust shalt thou return.
    Genesis 3:17-19

4. In the 28th chapter of Deuteronomy, we can read

30

about the blessings and curses of the Law. People who violated that Law encountered problems and economic depravity. Are the following curses from Deuteronomy 28 in your history and still working in your present?

But it shall come to pass, if thou wilt not hearken unto the voice of the LORD thy God, to observe to do all his commandments and his statutes which I command thee this day; that all these curses shall come upon thee, and overtake thee:

Cursed shalt thou be in the city, and cursed shalt thou be in the field.

Cursed shall be thy basket and thy store.

Thou shalt...plant a vineyard, and shalt not gather the grapes thereof.

Thine ox shall be slain before thine eyes, and thou shalt not eat thereof: thine ass shall be violently taken away from before thy face, and shall not be restored to thee: thy sheep shall be given unto thine enemies, and thou shalt have none to rescue them.

The fruit of thy land, and all thy labours, shall a nation which thou knowest not eat up; and thou shalt be only oppressed and crushed alway:

Thou shalt carry much seed out into the field, and shalt gather but little in; for the locust shall consume it.

Thou shalt plant vineyards, and dress them, but shalt neither drink of the wine, nor gather the grapes; for the worms shall eat them.

Thou shalt have olive trees throughout all thy

coasts, but thou shalt not anoint thyself with the oil; for thine olive shall cast his fruit.

Thou shalt beget sons and daughters, but thou shalt not enjoy them; for they shall go into captivity.

All thy trees and fruit of thy land shall the locust consume.

He shall lend to thee, and thou shalt not lend to him: he shall be the head, and thou shalt be the tail.

Therefore shalt thou serve thine enemies which the LORD shall send against thee, in hunger, and in thirst, and in nakedness, and in want of all things: and he shall put a yoke of iron upon thy neck, until he have destroyed thee.

Deuteronomy 28:15-17, 30-31, 33, 38-42, 44, 48

Your Attitude Determines Your Altitude

Now is the time to change! You must correct your views about your job and income. This is an important part of finding your field to harvest.

During my divorce and remarriage to Faye in 1975, I complained about my work and how poor my pay was. Then, one day I read the following verse in the Bible:

And whatsoever ye do in word or deed, do all in the name of the Lord Jesus, giving thanks to God and the Father by him.

Colossians 3:17

This Scripture revealed a big problem in my life. For years, many of my friends and I continually complained about our jobs.

I realized that I had never worked *in Jesus' Name.* From that moment on, I performed every weld on each car, proclaiming, "In Jesus' Name." Many times each minute for weeks, I repeated over my work, "In Jesus' Name." Suddenly one day, I noticed my sense of work had changed, because I was also giving thanks to God continually. Wow, what a change it was! After awhile, I grew to love my job. It even became a joy. Yet, nothing had changed except my attitude.

One of the greatest fallacies is that circumstances must change for joy to come. No! Right where you are, begin to conform your thinking, words, and actions to the Word of God. Then, joy will follow!

> In every thing give thanks: for this is the will of God
> in Christ Jesus concerning you.
>
> 1 Thessalonians 5:18

When you change your attitude, you change your altitude! Also remember:

> Death and life are in the power of the tongue: and
> they that love it shall eat the fruit thereof.
>
> Proverbs 18:21

Now you are on your way to washing your mentality by the Word, so God can prove His will for your life.

> And be not conformed to this world: but be ye
> transformed by the renewing of your mind, that ye may
> prove what is that good, and acceptable, and perfect,
> will of God.
>
> Romans 12:2

Renewing your mind to God's truth brings you into His will.

How can you do this? You renew your mind by washing it with the Word of God, which means reading the Bible and meditating on it, asking God how to apply it to your life.

> ...Christ also loved the church, and gave himself for it;
> *That he might sanctify and cleanse it with the washing of water by the word,*
> That he might present it to himself a glorious church, not having spot, or wrinkle, or any such thing; but that it should be holy and without blemish.
>
> Ephesians 5:25-27

We will discuss thinking and attitudes further in a later chapter.

How to Identify the Field God Planted for You

It is God's will for you to work and harvest the field of your dreams, which He planted for you to enjoy. To determine whether you have discovered God's field for you, ask yourself these questions:

1. In contrast to the curses, which we read earlier, do God's blessings in Deuteronomy 28 describe your life and work?

    > And it shall come to pass, if thou shalt hearken diligently unto the voice of the LORD thy God, to observe and to do all his commandments which I command thee this day, that the LORD thy God will set thee on high above all nations of the earth:
    > And all these blessings shall come on thee, and overtake thee, if thou shalt hearken unto the voice of the LORD thy God.

Blessed shalt thou be in the city, and blessed shalt thou be in the field.

Blessed shall be the fruit of thy body, and the fruit of thy ground, and the fruit of thy cattle, the increase of thy kine, and the flocks of thy sheep.

Blessed shall be thy basket and thy store.

Blessed shalt thou be when thou comest in, and blessed shalt thou be when thou goest out.

The LORD shall cause thine enemies that rise up against thee to be smitten before thy face: they shall come out against thee one way, and flee before thee seven ways.

The LORD shall command the blessing upon thee in thy storehouses, and in all that thou settest thine hand unto; and he shall bless thee in the land which the LORD thy God giveth thee.

And the LORD shall make thee plenteous in goods, in the fruit of thy body, and in the fruit of thy cattle, and in the fruit of thy ground, in the land which the LORD sware unto thy fathers to give thee.

The LORD shall open unto thee his good treasure, the heaven to give the rain unto thy land in his season, and to bless all the work of thine hand: and thou shalt lend unto many nations, and thou shalt not borrow.

And the LORD shall make thee the head, and not the tail; and thou shalt be above only, and thou shalt not be beneath; if that thou hearken unto the commandments of the LORD thy God, which I command thee this day, to observe and to do them:

> And thou shalt not go aside from any of the
> words which I command thee this day, to the
> right hand, or to the left, to go after other gods to
> serve them.
>
> Deuteronomy 28:1-8, 11-14

2. Simply consider the most fulfilling work you could do. Is that what you do now?

3. Are you in your element daily? Are you blossoming and expressing your giftings?

4. When you produce your daily tasks, do they self-perpetuate; or is every day a sense of never-ending drudgery?

5. At the end of the day, do you sense growth in your personal life's dream?

Right now, maybe you are thinking, *I am not experiencing anything from the field that God has planted for me.* If so, don't give up. It is out there for you and will fit you like a hand in a glove.

You may want to begin working toward your dreams on a part-time basis. Allow them to grow until you are fully experiencing them! In everything you do, always remember that your attitude, words, and actions in the present will affect your future!

Remember, if you obey God, all His blessings and promises are yours. No man can stop what God has declared for you. Your Heavenly Father wants to overtake you with His blessings so you cannot compare your latter days with your former. If you obey Him, He will bless you.

If you are not experiencing the blessings yet, there is a reason. Understand that for *every* effect, there is a cause. You see, an effect cannot take place in *any* arena without a cause. In the Bible, this principle of "cause and effect" is called "seedtime and harvest." If you can root out the cause of your lack, then release that which God originally intended, you can cause the effect He intends for you. That effect is blessings, wealth, fulfillment and prosperity in every area of your life.

You see, in writing to the Galatians, the Apostle Paul said:

> Christ hath redeemed us from the curse of the law, being made a curse for us: for it is written, Cursed is every one that hangeth on a tree:
> That the blessing of Abraham might come on the Gentiles through Jesus Christ; that we might receive the promise of the Spirit through faith.
> Galatians 3:13-14

The blessing of Abraham is, first, that you receive the promise of the Spirit through faith. Second, it is that you have the full person of the Spirit of God flowing in your life. Third, the blessing of Abraham is also that you have everything God promised in His covenant with Abraham. You have the right to receive God's blessings coming and going. Every enemy that rises against you will be smitten before your face and dispersed, according to Deuteronomy 28. Are you experiencing these promises? You can! Keep reading. Prepare yourself for the next chapter, as we launch further into the principle of Prophetic Vision.

4
Activate Your Dream Seeds

Continuing in the *Millionaire Mentality* principle of Prophetic Vision, let me assure you that you have everything at your disposal to accomplish your dreams. Why then are the graveyards of the world filled with aborted dreams? It need not be this way. Here, you will learn how to plant your dream seeds, so they will mature fully as God originally intended.

Today, many people have dreams in their spirits, which have not yet activated. Is this your situation? Have everyday events and challenges obscured your dream? Do you face circumstances that influence your vision to limit, bind, and restrain it? Perhaps you have attempted to accomplish your dream, but were unsuccessful. Don't let your enemy tempt you to shove your visions aside in frustration and say, "Forget it. This is too involved." This is *not* God's plan for you.

What Did God Originally Intend?

What then *is* God's intention for your life?

Man Is to Rule
To discover the answer to these questions, let's examine God's original dream for Adam and Eve.

> So God created man in his own image, in the image
> of God created he him; male and female created he them.

> And God blessed them, and God said unto them, *Be fruitful, and multiply, and replenish the earth, and subdue it: and have dominion* over the fish of the sea, and over the fowl of the air, and over every living thing that moveth upon the earth.
>
> Genesis 1:27-28

What an awesome responsibility this was! Think about what God dreamed for the first man and woman. In effect, He commanded them, saying, "I want you to start being fruitful. Multiply. Wherever you find loss in the earth, replenish it. Remake the entire earth, and subdue anything that is lawless. When you finish all this and the earth is the way it needs to be, I want you to rule over it. This is My dream for you. Everything I have created is under your influence. Adam, I invest within you the full authority and capacity to administer creation."

What did Adam do because of God's dream? He gave direction to the animals and named them. He imparted purpose to everything in existence. How did Adam do this? He operated his dream from a divine purpose and identity. You see, his identity was not in his humanity but born of God's original intention for mankind.

Actually, God destined *all* of mankind to rule, control, and take absolute dominion over his environment. We can see this in Psalm 8:4-6, which reveals our Heavenly Father's thoughts concerning man:

> What is man, that thou art mindful of him? and the son of man, that thou visitest him?
>
> For thou hast made him a little lower than the angels, and hast crowned him with glory and honour.
>
> Thou madest him to have dominion over the works

of thy hands; thou hast put all things under his feet:

Psalm 8:4-6

Here, we see that God created man in His image and bestowed glory and honor upon him.

Have you ever felt without honor because of other people's actions, attitudes, or motivations toward you? Please realize that this does not diminish God's thoughts about you. Change your thinking to conform to God's thoughts and His Word. We will further discuss your thinking in the next chapter.

You and I carry God's glory and honor within us. We are His children! I believe that God has so glorified us that it is the earth's privilege for us to walk on it. It is the air's privilege for us to breathe it. We are not debtors to oxygen, but oxygen is a debtor to us. I don't believe we owe money anything. However, money owes us everything, because money only exists for our use. Think about it. We are the purpose of money's existence. God has created you and me with glory, honor, and dignity. We live in the realm of dominion—designed to rule, not to be subject to another.

For example, consider a child's development. A baby knows only how to act humanly. Having recently come from God, he longs to express his freedom. Therefore, he screams loudly until he gets his own way. You see, he knows only that he has come to the earth to rule and be served. Adults then tell him, "No, no, that's not how it is in the real world." They condition him to become a servant of his environment and its systems and regulations, which, in turn, squash his entire motivation to create. Later, people might wonder why he lacks motivation. One reason is that when he was developing the ability to stand up and rule an environment, adults shut him up, sat him down, and told him he was wrong. Instead, what would have resulted if they had directed the child's motivation into the creative avenues of God?

Some actions that we interpret as rebellion in children really are not that at all. They simply are expressions of a spirit that does not believe others can contain and restrain it. I believe one of the greatest thefts is the educational process to which we subject our children. Are we training them to live according to what God has promised them? Are we teaching them to run this world because they have all God's blessings? For the vast majority of children, the answer to these questions is, "No." We don't educate them to rule, reign, and take dominion. Instead, we teach them to live subject to a ruling, conforming society, which dictates what they can do. As adults, then, they become disciplined with bondage, restrictions, and limitations instead of the limitless ability to rule.

Most of the psychology under which we live is not biblical wisdom. It steals from humanity the very roots and elements of our Godly dignity in creation. It takes from us the original intention to rule and take dominion in the earth. I believe our environment has so affected us that it feels illegal to think beyond the boundaries of our limitations. We are uncertain whether God wants us to explore these uncharted realms. However, the truth is that God says we can do all things when we represent and obey Him on the earth.

After this brief study of God's original intention for humanity, we see that He preprogrammed *every* man, woman, and child to rule. This includes you! Never forget that your Heavenly Father has preprogrammed you this way as He did Adam and Eve. Since God designed you to rule, then did He create the faculties within you to have this type of influence? Oh, yes, He did. He has provided everything you need to bear fruit, multiply, replenish, subdue, and take dominion. You see,

God's plan through Jesus Christ is to redeem you from your limitations to His limitless life, so you can rule in this earth. Before He made you, God envisioned your purpose within His being and created you with the abilities to achieve that purpose.

Now, you need to tap into and release those abilities to operate. It's time to identify what will stimulate the dream, which God has already sown in your spirit. What will move you to action? Realize this:

- You are the product of God's dream before creation.
- God designed all of creation to provide the opportunity for you to exercise your abilities and achieve His dreams within you.

Now, you must activate your dreams, instead of allowing them to lie dormant. Don't live as others do. God designed you to be different from the average person. How then shall we live?

Man Is to Reap Perpetual Harvests

As we read in Genesis 1:28, God's original design was for man to bear fruit, multiply, replenish, subdue, and dominate. Let's examine each of these aspects we are to fulfill.

Bear fruit. Being fruitful implies enjoying perpetual harvests. You see, my definition of *fruitful* is "the process of bringing seeds to maturity, harvesting, and producing more seeds from the harvest to create perpetual harvests." Fruitfulness does not mean that something merely bears fruit. Yes, there is fruit, but the fruit has seed, which creates new fruit, and the new fruit creates new seeds, and so on. It is a perpetuation, a continuum— not an end in itself.

Multiply. My definition of *multiply* is "to increase anything by duplicating itself." God designed us to duplicate. Consider business. No matter what field of business you may enter, it will not be an entirely original idea. (After all, even Christopher Columbus' radical idea of the world being round instead of flat was not really new. He stated that the inspired thought came from reading God's Word![1] For more information about this and other similar stories, read my book *It Only Takes One.*) It would behoove you to find a successful system that someone else has created and duplicate it.

You see, everything is a pattern of something else. This is why franchising does so well in the U.S.A. For example, Coca-Cola, Pepsi, and McDonald's Golden Arches now are worldwide. Why? They multiplied by duplicating themselves. Which people make a lot of money? Multipliers!

Replenish. *Replenish* means "to constantly supply refills to whatever becomes depleted." Instead of complaining about what is not working, God designed us to fill it up again. We dislike areas of vacuum in society and challenges with people groups. Well, God designed us to fix these problems. We are the answer to everything depleted in life.

Have you seen an area of depletion that bothers you? For instance, does the decay of a nearby city block grieve you? Does the demise of our nation's morals and values concern you? Does your heart break when you hear about abused or abandoned children or aborted babies? Does the loneliness of an elderly neighbor tug at your heart? Do you have compassion on a young mother down the street, who is dying of cancer? You must understand why you are here. God has put His children—including you and me—on this earth to replenish city blocks; to stand for His values; to save abused, abandoned, and aborted children; to love the elderly; to pray for the sick; and to meet the needs of this world. You are not here to complain about the problems. No, God created you to refill them to the full capacity according to His original intention and purpose.

God created you to make the difference. The world needs you to fill its gaps and mend its broken walls. I have heard it said, "Find a need and fill it." That's mankind's job.

Subdue. How do you *subdue?* My definition is "to bring all chaotic, lawless, aimless obstacles in subjection to your purpose by conquering." God gave you the gift of subduing. Therefore, you can conquer anything in His Name.

> Nay, in all these things we are more than conquerors through him that loved us.
>
> Romans 8:37

> But Jesus beheld them, and said unto them, With men this is impossible; but with God all things are possible.
>
> Matthew 19:26

Recently, I met the manager of an engineering group, which works for a large conglomerate of oil companies. Surprisingly, this manager is not an engineer himself. In fact, he did not even graduate from junior college. Yet, his annual salary is $125,000!

I asked how he could manage engineers and not understand what they do.

He replied, "I wouldn't want to waste my time. I don't have to understand what they do. I just need to get them to do what I tell them and make sure they know how to do it."

"Who gives your orders?" I asked.

"Someone who also doesn't know what they do!" he answered.

I realized he was right. The person who supervises this manager also has no idea how these systems work. His educational background is not engineering, either. He simply has the subduing responsibility of bringing these people under purpose and making sure they carry out his orders.

At this point, you may be thinking, *Why am I reading all this? I thought I was about to learn how to have a Millionaire Mentality.* Well, this is the root of it. Much of the *Millionaire Mentality* is recognizing that God designed you to bear fruit, multiply, replenish, subdue, and dominate. When you understand this, it's time to plant your dream seeds in fertile soil.

Dominate. Lastly, God made you to have *dominion*, that is, "to rule absolutely." However, sometimes you may feel like retreating from areas of challenge, because you feel ill equipped to influence the circumstances. Allow your faith to play an important role here. No matter how you feel, place your faith and trust in God, knowing that He designed you to influence *every* environment you encounter. Remember, His Word declares this, so it must be true.

God Is Our Source of Wealth

From the beginning, God intended to be our source of wealth. Please don't misunderstand. There is nothing wrong with working and earning an income, but this should not be all the revenue you receive. After all, God *does* say that we must provide for our families:

> But if any provide not for his own, and specially for those of his own house, he hath denied the faith, and is worse than an infidel.
>
> 1 Timothy 5:8

However, since God—not your job—is your source, don't limit your income to your job. God has other avenues through which He desires to prosper you. Yet, they *all* come from Him.

Suppose you say to your supervisor at work one day, "I

want to read Deuteronomy 28:1-14 to you. I expect all the blessings listed here to come from this corporation." Before you can finish reading, however, your manager probably will dock your pay, because you are wasting his time. Why? When you look closely at the blessings in Deuteronomy 28, God does not promise that your job will provide them. No, these blessings will come from *Him*.

Realize that no human being on this earth will pay you what you are worth. So, why do you expect it from people? Why don't you expect from God what He said you are worth? Your source is not humanity. Your source is God, so receive what you are worth from Heaven.

You might be thinking, *I don't know how to receive what I am due from Heaven.* This is a basic conflict of the Church. We don't understand our worth in Christ. Nor do we know how to receive God's blessings. Remember, our Heavenly Father sent His Son, Jesus, to die for us and has promised blessings to us. Yet, our minds revert to what our deceived forefathers have taught us. We choose to believe society, instead of the Word of God. You are what God declared you to be, and no one can diminish you. No one can steal enough from you that would cause God to lack.

Think about this. Jesus employed a thief to manage His money, yet He never complained of lack. What an acid test! Take a proven, known thief, give him complete control of all the money you earn, and never suffer lack in any area. Would we dare to do that? Probably many of us would not, because we still look to people as our sources instead of tapping into the resources of God. We will discuss this further in a later chapter.

Plant Your Dream Seeds

What can you do when you have dreams that appear far

beyond your human ability? Throughout the Bible, God's people had impossible dreams. Yet, I can almost hear the Lord saying to them and to you today, "I have made you and given these dream seeds to you. Now sow them, and watch what happens."

In the Bible, Elisha, the son of Shaphat, stopped plowing his field and sowed his life to become Prophet Elijah's servant. Then, when God took Elijah to Heaven, Elisha literally picked up Elijah's mantle and became the Prophet Elisha. He had sown his dream to be like Elijah, and then went on to perform twice as many miracles as Elijah. (You can read the story of Elisha in 1 Kings 19 through 2 Kings 13.)

King David had a consuming dream in his spirit—a vision for the dwelling place of God:

> Furthermore David the king said unto all the congregation, Solomon my son, whom alone God hath chosen, is yet young and tender, and the work is great: for the palace is not for man, but for the LORD God.
>
> Now I have prepared with all my might for the house of my God the gold for things to be made of gold, and the silver for things of silver, and the brass for things of brass, the iron for things of iron, and wood for things of wood; onyx stones, and stones to be set, glistering stones, and of divers colours, and all manner of precious stones, and marble stones in abundance.
>
> Moreover, because I have set my affection to the house of my God, I have of mine own proper good, of gold and silver, which I have given to the house of my God, over and above all that I have prepared for the holy house.
>
> 1 Chronicles 29:1-3

When David conquered all the enemy nations, he did not

48

simply desire more territory. No, he wanted to exercise his might for dominion, so he could build a house for God. All his days, he was willing to be a man of bloodshed, conquering and subduing. Something inside David caused him to sow for what he dreamed. We find that David's donation to the building of Solomon's temple was about a billion dollars in today's currency.

Today, Saudi Arabia is channeling tens of millions of dollars to build mosques around the world. Why? It is because the Saudis have a passion. How did they obtain the money to pursue their passion? They took hold of God's resource, oil, and started believing they had the right to control it. Saudi Arabia then joined several other oil-producing nations to form a cartel called OPEC (Organization of Petroleum Exporting Countries). Together they dictated the economy of the world by raising and lowering the prices and supply of oil according to how much money they wanted to make. They were simply acting like human beings. Today, they are taking dominion, and the rest of the world must respond to their decisions.

The decision-makers of the world are merely acting like humans. Where did they get their authority? It is from God. All humanity has this authority. However, we who are redeemed from the curse of the law have better promises. Not only do we have the promises God gave to all humanity, but we also have the covenant of Abraham. Beyond that, we have a more exceedingly precious covenant in Christ Jesus.

> ...The earth is the LORD'S, and the fulness thereof;
> the world, and they that dwell therein.
>
> Psalm 24:1

Now, we have not only the earth, which is the Lord's, and the fullness thereof, but we also have the delegated authority to use it according to God's purposes.

Expect God's Best Even in Negative Circumstances

Let every negative situation you face produce a Godly motivation for wealth. Then, extract the gold from each the crisis. For example, see how Israel did this. For hundreds of years, they had lived under bondage. Then, when Moses heard from God, he declared they would take Egypt's wealth when they left. They did.

> And the children of Israel did according to the word of Moses; and they borrowed of the Egyptians jewels of silver, and jewels of gold, and raiment:
> And the LORD gave the people favour in the sight of the Egyptians, so that they lent unto them such things as they required. And they spoiled the Egyptians.
> Exodus 12:35-36

Every time God set the Israelites free from bondage and impoverishment, they received huge economic breakthroughs. That's why in the Bible, the millions of Jews could carry wealth for three generations without ever working at paying jobs! Don't think that you will experience anything less. In my life, every time I have come free from limitation and control, great economic resources have followed the breakthroughs. It is a biblical pattern. The Bible declares:

> A good man leaves an inheritance for his children's children, but *a sinner's wealth is stored up for the righteous.*
> A poor man's field may produce abundant food, but injustice sweeps it away.
> Proverbs 13:22-23 (NIV)

How do we obtain sinners' wealth? Do we steal it from

them? Oh, no. You don't need to steal it, because God will cause them simply to give it to you. When will they do this? You will reap this kind of blessing when you plant the dream in your heart and tap into the giftings God has already placed within you!

Do you remember when Oral Roberts announced that he would die unless God provided a certain amount of funds (millions of dollars)? Many people, especially in the U.S.A., mocked him as a fool who was blaming God for his lack of money. No, this is a contemporary person who publicly declared that God *would make it happen.* Do you remember the result? The money came to him from a dog owner, who was a gambling unbeliever! In communion with God, Oral Roberts had set his dream before the Lord, saying, "God, this *has* to work." It did.

One of the greatest faculties you possess is the power to create. Maybe circumstances have suffocated and squashed this ability within you. It may now be frustrated, disappointed, and limited. Maybe you grew up in an environment, which told you, "This is impossible. It will never work."

Know that your history does not make any difference to your future. Only your dream and the seeds you activate matter. Remember, you don't have to activate a fully mature oak tree. You simply need to activate an acorn (or seed), because all the oak trees in the world start as tiny acorns.

You may have heard the American pioneer stories about Johnny Appleseed, whose real name was John Chapman (1774-1845). Reportedly, for 40 years, Johnny traveled the frontier, planting apple trees in wild nurseries and distributing apple seeds to settlers heading west. "He wanted one thing only—to carry the apple seeds of the East to the newly cleared lands of the West so that the pioneers might have the juicy fruit to eat."[2] When the settlers paid him money, "he gave it to the poor, bought religious books, or fed broken-down horses. More often they paid him in cast-off clothing or cornmeal."[3] Yet, he followed his dream. Then, before his death, Johnny Appleseed had the honor of seeing apple orchards span thousands of acres, which descended from his seedlings! One could say that he lived not by the question of how many seeds are in an apple, but how many apples are in a seed.

Don't simply see your dream seeds at face value. Envision their multiplied fruit!

America's Declaration of Independence states:

> We hold these truths to be self-evident, that all men are created equal, that they are endowed by their Creator with certain unalienable Rights, that among these are Life, Liberty and the pursuit of Happiness.

By the term *the pursuit of Happiness,* the signers "meant the right to own property and to have it safeguarded. It also meant the right to strive for the good of all people, not only for one's personal happiness."[4] Americans live in a society in which we have the right of ownership. This is not true in many places across the world. Why did God put Americans in such a free environment? The reason is so we can take the world for Christ!

You can look at life, trying to determine how many seeds are in each apple. On the other hand, you can choose to expand your vision to ponder how many apple *trees* are in every *seed.* Start thinking multiplication. Think about replenishing, subduing, and taking dominion. It's time to rule your environment. It is your right. No one on this earth can take it from you, because no earthly being gave it to you.

See the magnitude of your God! Take the limits off Him!

Now, pray this as you receive the *Millionaire Mentality* principle of Prophetic Vision:

God of Heaven, I recognize that in Your Word exists limitless resources and ability. In fact, You have created me limitless in my very nature, because You made me in Your image.

Father, I believe Your Word, which says that You created me to be a fruit producer, multiplier, replenisher, subduer, and dominator. You created and destined me to rule in this world and take dominion. I step into that anointing right now.

This world has no voice in my dream. My dream gives voice to this world. I am Your representative and ambassador for Christ, the temple of the Spirit of the Lord. According to Your Word, I have the right to live in glory, honor, and dignity, which magnify the God I serve.

Jesus, You have lifted me and released me to emulate Your life. Spirit of the Lord, reign through me. Move through me. Stir the dreams and Prophetic Visions within my heart as I plant them in Your hands. I expect to reap Your promised blessings and provisions, because I choose to obey and follow You with all my heart. In Jesus' Name. Amen.

5
Become Pregnant with God's Dream

It's time to get pregnant!

As you spend time fellowshipping with God, you become intimate with Him through His Holy Spirit. He then impregnates you with His dream! If you do not have a vision or cannot see how to achieve the vision you do have, then get intimate with God. Let Him fill you to overflowing with a clear direction of promise for your life! In this chapter, we will examine the third *Millionaire Mentality* principle: Pregnant Meditation. This key can change your life.

As a Man Thinks, So Is He

Accept the responsibility of the vision, which the Spirit of God has placed within your heart. Do this even if you do not know what it is yet. Recognize that you carry God's dream within you, and seek Him to discover it. Realize that your situation does not limit God. In fact, your present circumstances do not dictate the dream He establishes for your life. Instead, His dream will provide purpose for your life and literally free you from your challenges. Remember, God does not look at your situation today to determine what He can do with you tomorrow.

It's important to change your thinking. You see, unless you think correctly, you will not become impregnated with the dream and the mind of God. Proverbs 23:7 tells us:

For as he thinks in his heart, so is he....

Proverbs 23:7 (NKJV)

What a man thinks deep down in the innermost recesses of his being causes him to become what he thinks. This Scripture works for good and bad thoughts. It does not matter. The principle is the same.

For example, in an earlier chapter, I shared how on my miserable job, I began to thank and praise God with each weld. Soon, my work became a joy. On the negative side, countless men have left their wives and families after becoming obsessed with other women through Internet pornography, chat rooms, and E-mail. Thinking about being unfaithful caused them to fulfill their thoughts. Whether your thoughts are correct or not, you become what you think.

Many people allow their Prophetic Visions to go undone, because they focus on the lack of money. Yet, not one biblical reference exists in which God stopped moving because of the lack of finances. As we have discussed, He placed you on this earth to carry out His objectives. However, He does not give a vision to you and stop there. He also provides the means to accomplish it by pouring out wealth upon you. After all, you must have finances to accomplish His dream. This is why the Lord wants to develop the mindset in you that you can receive His wealth! He wants to remove the limits on your financial belief system, so you can fulfill His plans on earth.

This subject has burned within my spirit since November 1991 when the Lord instructed me to wage war on debt. He has impressed strongly upon my heart that He desires to pour out financial blessings upon His people. However, the greatest hindrance to this transfer of the world's wealth to the Body of Christ is their wrong beliefs. Christians think they are not worthy of great financial blessings, or they do not believe it is God's will for them to prosper. We must overcome these lies of the enemy.

You see, if you will change the way you *think,* you will change the way you *exist.* Too many people abort the dream of the Spirit by holding onto the reality of the natural realm. Many often fear dreams, because they appear too big and impossible compared to the circumstances. However, as we read earlier, the Bible warns that we cannot serve two masters. Either you must walk in the Spirit and pursue your dreams, or walk in the natural realm and reap the consequences of poverty.

> This I say then, Walk in the Spirit, and ye shall not fulfil the lust of the flesh.
>
> For the flesh lusteth against the Spirit, and the Spirit against the flesh: and these are contrary the one to the other: so that ye cannot do the things that ye would.
>
> But if ye be led of the Spirit, ye are not under the law.
>
> Galatians 5:16-18

You cannot be double-minded and expect to succeed.

> But let him ask in faith, nothing wavering. For he that wavereth is like a wave of the sea driven with the wind and tossed.
>
> For let not that man think that he shall receive any thing of the Lord.
>
> A double minded man is unstable in all his ways.
>
> James 1:6-8

Your dream must consume you. Then, God will provide the wealth to accomplish it.

The Holy Spirit Broods over You

In the first two verses of the Bible, we read:

> In the beginning God (prepared, formed, fashioned,) and created the heavens and the earth.
> The earth was without form and an empty waste, and darkness was upon the face of the very great deep. *The Spirit of God was moving, (hovering, brooding) over the face of the waters.*
>
> Genesis 1:1-2 (AMP)

Who was God when He created the heavens and the earth? Since all that He is and does is perfect, God does not create anything that is void, formless, and lacking. Therefore, something must have happened between Genesis 1:1 and 1:2 to cause this. That's when I believe the fall of Lucifer occurred, and Satan became God's number-one enemy. Otherwise, how could the earth have been void and without form? How could darkness have been upon the face of the deep, when the Bible says that in God there is no darkness?

> This then is the message which we have heard of him, and declare unto you, that God is light, and in him is no darkness at all.
>
> 1 John 1:5

Therefore, this must have been when Lucifer and one-third of the angels fell, which resulted in a chaotic environment. (For more information about this event, please read Isaiah 14, Ezekiel 28, and Revelation 12. My book *Conquering Your Unseen Enemies* also explains the story of the angels' fall.)

Then, in Genesis 1:2, with the original dream of God, the Holy Spirit entered the chaos and hovered over it. The word *hover* is like the mother hen, which sits on her eggs and broods over them until they hatch into chicks. She envisions one form (eggs) becoming another (chicks), and she is willing to do whatever it takes to bring her eggs into the next form. Similarly, the Holy Spirit comes with God's original intention and dream for your life. Then, He says, "I am willing to incubate your life until I bring you forth into what I intend you to be and to do."

Release your thoughts from life as it now appears into that which God has always thought, purposed, and dreamed for you. What is on God's heart concerning you? What is in His mind? What has He been thinking and dreaming about you?

The Apostle Paul wrote:

> Who hath saved us, and called us with an holy calling, not according to our works, but according to his own *purpose and grace, which was given us* in Christ Jesus *before the world began.*
>
> 2 Timothy 1:9

The thoughts of God for your life did not occur when you were born. His will concerning you has absolutely nothing to do with your natural birth. Before the world began in Genesis 1:1, God called you for a purpose in Christ Jesus. He dreamed of you, purposed you, and had you in His Son before He created the heavens and the earth!

I believe the most beautiful women on the face of the earth are those who are physically pregnant. They glow. Carrying life inside does something in their spirits. The spark of incubation and growth of new life surges through the entire fabric of their beings.

You need to be pregnant spiritually, whether you are a man or woman. Carrying the energizing life of God's dream within your spirit invigorates your entire life. It's easy to recognize people who are fulfilling their dreams. It does not matter what they face. Nothing is too big for them to handle. However, for those who live only in the present—in the frustrations of today—nearly every little problem appears insurmountable.

Too many people in our society focus on the simple challenges of everyday life. That's not how God intends for you to live. He wants you to live the dream He had in mind for you even before you existed. The psalmist declared about God:

> For you created my inmost being; you knit me together in my mother's womb.
>
> I praise you because I am fearfully and wonderfully made; your works are wonderful, I know that full well.
>
> My frame was not hidden from you when I was made in the secret place. When I was woven together in the depths of the earth,
>
> your eyes saw my unformed body. All the days ordained for me were written in your book before one of them came to be.
>
> Psalm 139:13-16 (NIV)

Your Heavenly Father has a plan for you! When you become an incubator of that dream, all things work together for good, and your spirit soars with hope in God. He promises His children:

> And we know that all things work together for good to them that love God, to them who are the called according to his purpose.
>
> Romans 8:28

> Return to your fortress, O prisoners of hope; even
> now I announce that I will restore twice as much to you.
>
> Zechariah 9:12 (NIV)

You must renew your hope even now that God will restore you and breathe new life into your being.

Contrast this with a person with a "peanut brain." This is someone who thinks small—only about what he can see. Ask him, "What will you do today?"

He will reply, "Oh, I'll get up, get dressed, eat breakfast, brush my teeth, and go to work."

"Then what will you do?" you might ask.

"Put in my time," he will say, "take a break, put in my time, eat lunch, put in my time, take a break, put in my time, and go back home."

"Then what?"

"Yell at the kids, eat dinner, look at the paper, watch TV, and go to bed. Then, I'll wake up tomorrow, and start over."

This mundane, limited existence is *not* the life God dreamed and purposed for us before creation! No, we need to launch out, go over the edge, and allow Him to start revealing His larger dream.

By the impregnation of God's dream, I do not mean what the world has to offer: A better job, houses, cars, and worldly possessions. I do not refer to making money, having it, or spending it. I am not writing about what *man* can do. This is about discovering what is in God's mind and what *He* can do in your life. After all, nothing else is significant. This is the foundation of a *Millionaire Mentality*. The purpose of God is not according to our works. So let's settle this issue here. No matter how hard man works, how much he endeavors, or how strong his willpower is, God does not tie His purpose to man and his works.

God's dream is the most valuable entity in all of creation. Nothing is more influential or powerful. Nothing compares with what God thinks about you. What He had in mind about you before creation is the highest, most significant life you will ever tap into. When you discover the mind of God, everything else will follow it. Let God dream big inside you.

Big Dreams in Impossible Circumstances

Throughout the Bible, God's people carried out His dreams for their lives despite the odds. Let's examine Joseph's dream. At age 17, Jacob's favorite son, Joseph, dreamed of his brothers' sheaves bowing down to his (Genesis 37:7). When he shared it with his brothers, they hated him even more. Conspiring to rid themselves of his dreams, they threw Joseph into a pit, then sold him into slavery. He landed in an Egyptian prison. Eventually, however, Joseph grew extremely prosperous and powerful— second only to Pharaoh. He became ruler of Egypt and lived in the palace.

> And Pharaoh said unto his servants, Can we find such a one as this is, a man in whom the Spirit of God is?
> And Pharaoh said unto Joseph, Forasmuch as God hath showed thee all this, there is none so discreet and wise as thou art:
> Thou shalt be over my house, and according unto thy word shall all my people be ruled: only in the throne will I be greater than thou.
> And Pharaoh said unto Joseph, See, I have set thee over all the land of Egypt.
> And Pharaoh took off his ring from his hand, and put it upon Joseph's hand, and arrayed him in vestures of

fine linen, and put a gold chain about his neck;

And he made him to ride in the second chariot which he had; and they cried before him, Bow the knee: and he made him ruler over all the land of Egypt.

And Pharaoh said unto Joseph, I am Pharaoh, and without thee shall no man lift up his hand or foot in all the land of Egypt.

Genesis 41:38-44

Years later in the midst of a famine, Joseph's position enabled him to provide for his father and brothers. Thus, he saved them from starvation.

What a long way from the pit Joseph came! However, did you ever stop to think that Joseph's apparently impossible circumstances were actually part of God's fulfillment of his dream? This teaches us not to become discouraged when challenges come our way. Instead, we must accept and focus on God's plan for our lives.

Moses accepted God's vision for his life as the Israelites' deliverer from bondage. However, he then tried to accomplish it with his own strength by supposition. Today, we sometimes operate similarly by acting on our own assumptions.

And Moses was learned in all the wisdom of the Egyptians, and was mighty in words and in deeds.

And when he was full forty years old, it came into his heart to visit his brethren the children of Israel.

And seeing one of them suffer wrong, he defended him, and avenged him that was oppressed, and smote the Egyptian:

For he *supposed* his brethren would have understood how that God by his hand would deliver them: but they understood not.

Acts 7:22-25

Moses thought the rest of the Israelites had heard from God, too, but they had not. You see, a dream and vision from God gives to you a private line with God.

> And the next day he showed himself unto them as they strove, and would have set them at one again, saying, Sirs, ye are brethren; why do ye wrong one to another?
> But he that did his neighbour wrong thrust him away, saying, Who made thee a ruler and a judge over us?

Acts 7:26-27

Now, Moses had the answer to this question, for he was indeed to be the ruler and judge over Israel. However, he could not express this, because they would not hear it.

Jesus said:

> But blessed are your eyes, for they see: and your ears, for they hear.

Matthew 13:16

Many people see yet do not understand. They hear but have no consciousness of the significance.

Because the Israelites did not understand Moses' vision, the dream in him withered. They temporarily lost the blessings it would have provided. As a result, two entire generations of Israelites died. First, a generation died when Moses acted in supposition and the people did not understand that he was their deliverer. The second generation died as Israel wandered in the wilderness. It took 80 years for a new generation to come into the Promised Land.

Impossible circumstances and chaotic atmospheres usually surround God's dreams. When fulfilling God's dreams, most people become sidetracked into logjams of activity or other distractions. For example, let's say that you are praying in fellowship with God and starting to perceive His vision. Then, a challenge presents itself. Now, instead of capturing and running with the dream that controls you, you give your attention, focus, prayer life, and your entire effort to this situation. Suddenly, the question of whether your dream will manifest hinges upon this challenge.

You probably know people who are continually in conflict. They live from one tragedy to the next, from worry to worry, from anxiety to anxiety, and from frustration to frustration. They do not see a broader picture and go from glory to glory as God intends:

> But we all, with open face beholding as in a glass the glory of the Lord, are changed into the same image from glory to glory, even as by the Spirit of the Lord.
>
> 2 Corinthians 3:18

If you will run with God's dream, your challenges will work out. Why? Do you remember Romans 8:28, which we read earlier?

> And we know that all things work together for good to them that love God, to them who are the called according to his purpose.
>
> Romans 8:28

When you are following in His purpose, God orchestrates your circumstances. You do not have to tend them yourself. No longer must you occupy your mind with challenges.

Instead, God's dream within you must be your all-consuming motivation. His vision must be the overriding, presiding purpose in your life. You need to breathe, live, move, and have your being in it.

> That they should seek the Lord, if haply they might feel after him, and find him, though he be not far from every one of us:
> For in him we live, and move, and have our being; as certain also of your own poets have said, For we are also his offspring.
>
> Acts 17:27-28

Your vision is bigger than your life and what you can do alone. If you do not focus your entire being on God and His dream, you will find yourself trusting in the arm of the flesh as Moses first did. Then, your own fear can become a limiting factor.

After the Holy Spirit moved upon the face of the waters (Genesis 1:2), what happened?

> And God said, Let there be light; and there was light.
>
> Genesis 1:3

From chaos, God incubated His dream and spoke it forth. The Word of His power holds everything together.

No matter how chaotic your situation may be, God has a dream for you. From that dream, He can speak and give it direction. Your challenges do not matter, whether they are marital disharmony, financial destruction, physical infirmities, or social conflicts. Regardless of your circumstances, God's dream for you is big enough to deliver you from them. However, you must not look at or dwell upon the factors that bind you. Instead, look to the God who called you with a purpose even before your birth.

Think again about Abraham. Because of his faith, God told Abraham that He would bless all the families on earth:

> It was not through law that Abraham and his offspring received the promise that he would be heir of the world, but through the righteousness that comes by faith.
> Romans 4:13 (NIV)

Abraham became the heir of the world. Remember, because you now partake in the blessings of Abraham, you, too, are an heir of the world. God has destined you to rule, influence, control, and have absolute dominion. You must begin to think like it!

God's Dream for You

You might be thinking, *I'm reading* Millionaire Mentality. *I would be blessed, if I had a million dollars.* This is not a mentality of accumulation but of delegation. Don't live with the mindset of what you can accumulate to satisfy your flesh. You could lose it all in an afternoon. God is not a god of accumulation. He is the God who commands us to delegate, rule, control, and take dominion. Meditate on God's purpose for you since before the foundation of the world. Enlarge the capacity of your dream in Him. Realize that eternity is hanging on God's dreams for you!

Joseph stepped beyond the limitation of his bondage into the liberation of the dream, which God had given to him. Your liberation will not result from circumstances working together for you on earth. No, your liberation will come, because your dream is bigger than the earth. Freedom lies within your dream. It does not come from successful activities but from the limitless dream in your heart. Motivation does not occur when something goes your way. It comes when you see everything get out of your way! That's when something bigger than you will start to stir inside your spirit. So live beyond your circumstances. Take what God births in you—the dream seed of His revelation—and let it incubate. Brood over and meditate upon it until it forms within you who Christ is and what He wants you to do.

Remember, you must sow your dreams even in contrary environments. Don't ever wait for natural circumstances to work. If you do, this can disillusion and frustrate you. The Bible declares:

> Hope deferred maketh the heart sick: but when the desire cometh, it is a tree of life.
>
> Proverbs 13:12

When you expect earthly results on a horizontal plane and hope in natural results, you set yourself up to become disappointed and discouraged. On the other hand, when you live in the vertical plane of God's dream, circumstances work together perfectly, according to His plan.

You might be asking, *How can I live this way?*

Keep living in the future of your dreams.

Well, but what about today?

Today is only the product of yesterday. Tomorrow is where you need to live. Yes, you have faith for today, but your vision is for tomorrow. This is a different mindset.

God's dream is greater than what you can see with your natural eyes. You must live beyond the apparent. Live beyond today's frustrations. You see, you can live in the present and be miserable. Alternatively, you can live in God's dream and cause your present to serve His future purpose. Take what you have in your hand today, and make it serve your future. The Bible commands:

> Beat your plowshares into swords, and your pruninghooks into spears: let the weak say, I am strong.
>
> Joel 3:10

Beat your normal environment into a servant to fulfill the purpose of God. Allow the dream within you to change your environment. Let your spirit rise above the ordinary to soar in God. Take the average over the edge. Never forget: You are to live, think, breathe, move, and have your existence in His dream arena. Be an incubator of God's dreams.

The Apostle Paul wrote:

> But we speak the wisdom of God in a mystery, even the hidden wisdom, which God ordained before the world unto our glory:
>
> Which none of the princes of this world knew: for had they known it, they would not have crucified the Lord of glory.
>
> But as it is written, Eye hath not seen, nor ear heard, neither have entered into the heart of man, the things which God hath prepared for them that love him.
>
> But God hath revealed them unto us by his Spirit: for the Spirit searcheth all things, yea, the deep things of God.
>
> For what man knoweth the things of a man, save the spirit of man which is in him? even so the things of God knoweth no man, but the Spirit of God.
>
> Now we have received, not the spirit of the world,

but the spirit which is of God; that we might know the
things that are freely given to us of God.

1 Corinthians 2:7-12

Paul did not preach according to his experiences. No, he
spoke God's revelation from before the foundation of the earth,
preceding Genesis 1:1. He captured and communicated God's
wisdom from the ages before creation. Paul said that if the
demonic princes and strongholds, which govern this world,
had known, they would not have crucified Jesus. Neither does
man—through his faculties of reason, sight, and hearing—
possess the capacity to know what God has prepared for those
who love Him. Only the Holy Spirit knows the things of God.

For by grace are ye saved through faith; and that not
of yourselves: it is the gift of God:
Not of works, lest any man should boast.
For we are his workmanship, created in Christ Jesus
unto good works, which God hath before ordained that
we should walk in them.

Ephesians 2:8-10

You see, those who boast say, "I have accomplished and
achieved." However, those who walk in grace say, "I have
received God's free gift." We are to take the dream seeds, which
God freely gave and revealed to us, and bring them into existence.
Inside us, these seeds start forming, growing, and revealing
what is to come. Then, we need to become incubators and
solidifiers until God's dreams manifest.

Never forget: All that God purposed for your life existed
before the foundation of the earth; and the dreams, which the
Holy Spirit reveals, He gives *freely*. Nothing is more valuable
than God's gifts. You cannot raise enough money to pay Him

adequately for what He freely gives. It does not matter how much money, effort, work, strength, or stress you exert. God says, "My purpose for your life is independent of your works. My free gift is more than you alone could ever earn in your entire lifetime."

Now, quiet your spirit as you answer these important questions. What dream has God given to you? What revelation, from before the foundation of the earth, have you discovered? When you sit in God's throne room—in fellowship and communion with Him without shame, guilt, or inferiority—what do you see? What dream does God unveil before your eyes? What has He set in eternity for you? Maybe you are thinking, *I don't have one of those. I didn't know one existed for me.* Oh, but it does indeed exist for you. God has always had your dream in His mind. It's time for *you* to get it into *yours!*

Record the Vision and Keep It before Your Eyes

When the vision comes, expect your life to change. Habakkuk declared:

> I will stand my watch
> And set myself on the rampart,
> And watch to see what He will say to me,
> And what I will answer when I am reproved.
> Then the LORD answered me and said:
> Write the vision
> And make it plain on tablets,
> That he may run who reads it.
> For the vision is yet for an appointed time;
> But at the end it will speak, and it will not lie.
> Though it tarries, wait for it;
> Because it will surely come,

It will not tarry.

Habakkuk 2:1-3 (NKJV)

When God's vision comes to you, it will correct your thinking. Be sure to record the vision and keep it before your eyes and, if necessary, the eyes of others. Never allow it to lose its significance in your life.

Don't let the distractions of this world cause you to lose focus. These include advertising campaigns, sales gimmicks, and humanistic promotions. Jesus warned:

> And the cares of this world, and the deceitfulness of riches, and the lusts of other things entering in, choke the word, and it becometh unfruitful.
>
> And these are they which are sown on good ground; such as hear the word, and receive it, and bring forth fruit, some thirtyfold, some sixty, and some an hundred.
>
> Mark 4:19-20

If you don't keep your focus on your vision, your enemy will entice you through things and people, saying, "Follow me." In this way, he will tempt you to veer off course. If you submit, then you will not know the joy of fulfillment. You see, God did not design you to find fulfillment in these arenas. This never has been—and never will be—God's plan for you.

When you find God's dream for your life, let it correct and reprove you. Allow it to bring you to honesty. Give it room to deal with the areas of your life that you count significant and valuable. Let it break your outer man and affect you internally.

When a man truly has a dream, in the end, the dream has the man. It becomes his only focus—as if nothing else exists. Many people are still in the first stage, saying, "I will have a dream. I will hear it." This is not good enough. You must hear the dream, seize it, and allow it to change your thinking. Let it rearrange your entire being, so you can focus on God's eternal picture. Once His dream impregnates you, you no longer have it; it has you. If you let the vision have you, then you are no longer yourself. Now, you and the dream are one. No one can disconnect a person from his God-given dream.

Although Joseph's brothers tried, they could not separate him from his dream. You see, they were not trying to throw Joseph into the pit. It was his dream they desired to dispose of. However, since his dream was in his body, they threw Joseph's body into the pit.

> And his brethren said to him, Shalt thou indeed reign over us? or shalt thou indeed have dominion over us? And they hated him yet the more for his dreams, and for his words.
>
> And when they saw him afar off, even before he came near unto them, they conspired against him to slay him.
>
> And they said one to another, Behold, this dreamer cometh.
>
> Come now therefore, and let us slay him, and cast him into some pit, and we will say, Some evil beast hath devoured him: and we shall see what will become of his dreams.
>
> Genesis 37:8, 18-20

Likewise, it was not simply Joseph who went to prison or to the palace. It was also the dream in his body.

Pray in the Spirit to Receive God's Answer

You need to ask God His purpose for your life. Get His dream. Openly declare, "God, I cannot live without Your vision for my life. There is no reason for existing, if I don't discover why I am here on this earth." Then be a receiver, an incubator.

How do you get God's vision? How does it come into your spirit? Jesus said:

> God is a Spirit: and they that worship him must worship him in spirit and in truth.
>
> John 4:24

You receive the revelation of God's dream for your life by fellowshipping with Him in the Spirit. To do this, you need to pray in the Holy Spirit. I love the language of the Spirit of God. Although, I cannot understand it, it changes my entire being.

> For he that speaketh in an unknown tongue speaketh not unto men, but unto God: for no man understandeth him; howbeit in the spirit he speaketh mysteries [God's divine secrets].
>
> 1 Corinthians 14:2

When I pray in my native tongue, it is from the arena of my understanding. However, when I pray with the Spirit of God, I am praying in the arena of discovery. It is beyond the threshold of anything I could ever imagine. These are not possibility prayers but absolute realities. How can this be? It is because I am praying according to the mind and purpose of God. I am praying what God already has done in Heaven. As I pray in the Spirit, God reveals the answer to me in the form of a picture or perception.

> Wherefore let him that speaketh in an unknown tongue pray that he may interpret.

For if I pray in an unknown tongue, my spirit prayeth, but my understanding is unfruitful.

What is it then? I will pray with the spirit, and I will pray with the understanding also: I will sing with the spirit, and I will sing with the understanding also.

1 Corinthians 14:13-15

God has designed us to speak in the language of His Spirit and become pregnant with His dreams.

Millionaire Mentality has nothing to do with having more money in your wallet or bank account. It has to do with your mindset and the capacity to hear and receive from the mind of Christ. Listen to Him and allow Him to teach you. Earlier, we read part of the following passage in the Bible:

Come ye near unto me, hear ye this; I have not spoken in secret from the beginning; from the time that it was, there am I: and now the Lord GOD, and his Spirit, hath sent me.

Thus saith the LORD, thy Redeemer, the Holy One of Israel; I am the LORD thy God which teacheth thee to profit, which leadeth thee by the way that thou shouldest go.

Isaiah 48:16-17

These verses reveal that prosperity, increase, and success in life is a combination of teaching and leading. It is not an event. For example, in the workplace, we know that we cannot qualify for certain jobs until we learn specific fundamentals of those businesses or technologies. As we receive teaching from others with experience in these fields, we practice our new knowledge and skills. Eventually, then, we become proficient. Thus, as we accept teaching, we progress into deeper levels of experience.

This is God's desire for us in every area of life. He wants to teach us how to experience deeper levels of His blessings. God will teach you to profit and lead you in fulfilling His plan for your life. First, however, you must be willing to accept His teaching and then follow it. When you do, you will release wealth that will run to fulfill your prophetic purpose. Stay alert in prayer to recognize the leading of the Holy Spirit. Then follow His voice.

The Final Proof

No matter what you do, be certain that you do not allow your dream-driven life to violate the proven principles and examples in God's Word. Let it be the final proof in all you do. For example, follow God's Word regarding worry. You cannot receive the wisdom of God while the worries of everyday life occupy your mind. Instead, you must let the peace of God rule.

> Be careful for nothing; but in every thing by prayer and supplication with thanksgiving let your requests be made known unto God.
> And the peace of God, which passeth all understanding, shall keep your hearts and minds through Christ Jesus.
>
> Philippians 4:6-7

You must never allow an anxious thought to enter and stay in your mind.

Jesus said:

> Therefore I tell you, do not worry about your life,

what you will eat or drink; or about your body, what you will wear. Is not life more important than food, and the body more important than clothes?

Look at the birds of the air; they do not sow or reap or store away in barns, and yet your heavenly Father feeds them. Are you not much more valuable than they?

Matthew 6:25-26 (NIV)

Anchor your faith in the Bible's simple and practical truth: "IT IS WRITTEN!" Keep the Word of God in your heart at all times:

This book of the law shall not depart out of thy mouth; but thou shalt meditate therein day and night, that thou mayest observe to do according to all that is written therein: for then thou shalt make thy way prosperous, and then thou shalt have good success.

Joshua 1:8

Success Is Found in Your Daily Routine

Many say their dreams are "pie in the sky," believing that they will never happen. Have you ever heard anyone say that he will follow his dreams, "When my ship comes home," meaning when he gets rich? This type of thinking is very dangerous. The reason for concern is that every day around you, harvests are yours to reap. Daily, therefore, you should be moving in or toward your field to reap it. You see, your daily routine will cause you either to fail or succeed. The mentality of leaving your life to fate or "whatever comes" will set you up for failure. This is a sure way to avoid fulfilling your dream. You must have a take-charge attitude and lifestyle.

Daily, you must establish a routine of harnessing your mind

in relationship to time, correct judgments, and actions. The following Scripture has been a great measuring rod in my life:

> Whoso keepeth the commandment shall feel no evil thing: and a wise man's heart discerneth both time and judgment.
> Because to every purpose there is time and judgment, therefore the misery of man is great upon him.
>
> Ecclesiastes 8:5-6

If you are experiencing frustration and a never-ending drone of misery in your daily routine, it is time to modify it! Without *radical* change, however, you will continue operating in the same way. Then you will reap similar harvests over and over.

Now is the time to renew your mind. Remember, God is carrying out His purpose. Realize that He ties the purpose of your existence to His timing and decisions. Daily get your mind in gear. All of creation is waiting for you to renew your mind so you can take charge of your environment.

> The creation waits in eager expectation for the sons of God to be revealed.
>
> Romans 8:19

In the following Scripture you can experience a personal renovation of your mind. As you keep the Word of God foremost in your thoughts and speech, you change. It is like stripping old paint from an antique chair: You remove layer by layer until the original wood fully emerges. Then, in its restored condition the true value of the antique is clear. Remember:

> And be not conformed to this world: but be ye

transformed by the renewing of your mind, that ye may prove what is that good, and acceptable, and perfect, will of God.

Romans 12:2

To prove and see the Word of God fully manifest in your life, you must renew your mind! The daily pursuit of a renewed mind will cause you to experience God's awesome Word in action. Truth will stand every test!

Once you fully live His dream, we might need to change *Millionaire Mentality* to *Billionaire Mentality*!

Please pray this as we close our discussion on Pregnant Meditation:

Father God, Your Word clarifies that my thinking is critical. Please help me to renew my mind, to conform it not to the world but according to the truth in Your Word. Help me to rely on You and not to worry, fall into fear, or become distracted with the cares of this world.

Lord, restore me and breathe new life into me. Impregnate me with Your vision for my life as I become more intimate with You. Help me to obey Your Word by praying in the Holy Spirit and with my understanding. Let my prayers be fruitful to accomplish that which You desire.

Strengthen me so I am not double-minded. Help me to focus all that I have and all that I am on You and Your Prophetic Vision. Father, let me live, move, and have my being in You. Cause me to become an incubator of Your dream seeds. When challenges come, let me not become discouraged. Help me to remember that when

I follow Your Purpose, You will orchestrate my circumstances. Energize me with renewed hope that Your dreams for me WILL come to pass. In Jesus' Name. Amen.

6
Proclaim God's Words
to Release Wealth

We began our study of the *Millionaire Mentality* principles with the Purpose of wealth. Then we progressed to the principles of God's Prophetic Vision for your life and Pregnant Meditation. What is the purpose of wealth? It is to establish God's covenant. What is your Prophetic Vision? This is God's plan for your life, which He conceived before the foundation of the world. How do you discover the way to achieve His objectives? You allow the Holy Spirit to impregnate you with power and wisdom.

The next *Millionaire Mentality* principle is Proclamation. This is declaring that your vision will manifest and the provisions will flow into your life. Few people recognize the power of this biblical principle.

Recognize the Creative Power of Proclamation

To release your provision, you must proclaim your dream or vision. What can you accomplish through a proclamation? To discover this answer, let's examine the results of God's own Words. The first chapter of Genesis describes how God spoke the world into existence. Simply by the power of His Words, God created light, the sky or Heavens, the earth, seas, vegetation, the sun, the moon, stars, and animals. How could His Word have such power? It is because God and His Word are one.

In the beginning was the Word, and *the Word was with God, and the Word was God.*

The same was in the beginning with God.

All things were made by him; and without him was not any thing made that was made.

In him was life; and the life was the light of men.

And the light shineth in darkness; and the darkness comprehended it not.

And the Word was made flesh, and dwelt among us, (and we beheld his glory, the glory as of the only begotten of the Father,) full of grace and truth.

John 1:1-5, 14

While we may not fully comprehend it, this passage explains that God and Jesus are the Word. Their Words, then, contain all the power and glory of God and Jesus.

Furthermore, the Bible states that God's spoken Word is still effective:

God, who at sundry times and in divers manners spake in time past unto the fathers by the prophets,

Hath in these last days spoken unto us by his Son, whom he hath appointed heir of all things, by whom also he made the worlds;

Who being the brightness of his glory, and the express image of his person, and *upholding all things by the word of his power,* when he had by himself purged our sins, sat down on the right hand of the Majesty on high.

Hebrews 1:1-3

Upholding means that God's spoken Word (*Rhema* in Hebrew) is the binding force by which God holds everything together. This simple truth literally holds you together physically!

Words are the tools God uses to create. He holds everything together by His Word. The natural man may not understand this, because God said:

> For my thoughts are not your thoughts, neither are your ways my ways, saith the LORD.
> For as the heavens are higher than the earth, so are my ways higher than your ways, and my thoughts than your thoughts.
>
> Isaiah 55:8-9

Since God made us in His image, we have His creative power in our words. This is the power of proclamation.

Also, when you proclaim in alignment with God's purpose—not according to appearances—your mind then begins to conform to His thoughts. You see, when the Word of God comes, it corrects. The truth in the Word exposes your errors. In contrast, you recognize wrong perspectives and ungodly attitudes. With truth comes reproof.

> All Scripture is God-breathed and is useful for teaching, rebuking, correcting and training in righteousness,
> so that the man of God may be thoroughly equipped for every good work.
>
> 2 Timothy 3:16-17

God's Word equips us to carry out His vision for our lives.

Are You Declaring Your Belief?

Do you declare what you believe? If you do, what happens? Does God affirm the words you speak? If not, then what you believe may be wrong. There are many very sincere people who are sincerely deceived. *Sincerity is not an earmark of truth.* Remember, even the demons sincerely believe that Jesus is Lord.

> Thou believest that there is one God; thou doest well:
> the devils also believe, and tremble.
>
> James 2:19

In traveling around the world, I have met many kinds of people. Some of the most sincere are Muslims. They are earnest, committed, loyal, and faithful. However, when I ask them to pray to Muhammad for healing, the diseases persist in spite of their words. They also have no permanent assurance of salvation based upon the confession of their faith. The reason is because they do not believe God's *true* Word. Therefore, their sincerity does not induce God to bring them to salvation. What does? They must have a believing heart with faith in the Truth. What does faith consist of? Faith is a combination of heart belief, mouth declaration, and corresponding actions of obedience to God.

> That if thou shalt *confess with thy mouth* the Lord
> Jesus, and shalt *believe in thine heart* that God hath raised
> him from the dead, thou shalt be saved.
> For with the heart man believeth unto righteousness;
> and with the mouth confession is made unto salvation.
>
> Romans 10:9-10

> For as the body without the spirit is dead, so *faith
> without works is dead also.*
>
> James 2:26

This is for everyone. We must declare our faith and speak the truth.

Are you obeying God and passing His tests regarding your words; or are your words negative and full of defeat?

Do you say, "Oh, God, I cannot take any more"?

If so, He will respond: "Then, I cannot give any more to you."

Do not adopt the mindset that the pressures are too great, or your challenges are more than you can handle. This is not true. God promises:

> There hath no temptation taken you but such as is common to man: but God is faithful, who will not suffer you to be tempted above that ye are able; but will with the temptation also make a way to escape, that ye may be able to bear it.
>
> 1 Corinthians 10:13

Do not compare your strength to your conflict. Weigh God's strength against the challenge. The Apostle Paul declared about Jesus:

> But he [Jesus] said to me, "My grace is sufficient for you, for my power is made perfect in weakness." Therefore I will boast all the more gladly about my weaknesses, so that Christ's power may rest on me.
>
> 2 Corinthians 12:9 (NIV)

The day you declare, "I cannot deal with this," is the day you become trapped. When this happens, no one can free you. Your only way of escape then is to bow your knee to God, and seek His divine intervention.

Facing conflict can cause frustration, disappointment, disillusionment, and discouragement to set in. Because you feel as though you cannot handle any more, you simply want to quit. The pressures are too great, the day is too long, and the distress is insurmountable. However, the fact is, God uses the pressures to see if you will live by His Word. The Scriptures warn that if you cannot run with footmen, how then can you run with horsemen? If you feel defeated in ankle-deep water, how can you ever hope to swim?

> If thou hast run with the footmen, and they have wearied thee, then how canst thou contend with horses? and if in the land of peace, wherein thou trustedst, they wearied thee, then how wilt thou do in the swelling of Jordan?
>
> Jeremiah 12:5

Proclaim the Finances for the Vision

Think about Job's challenges in the Bible. During all his suffering, he had many opportunities to curse God and die. However, he refused to do so. Job sustained his integrity before God. He passed the test when he vowed and proclaimed God's Word, saying:

> Thou shalt make thy prayer unto him, and he shall hear thee, and thou shalt pay thy vows.
> Thou shalt also decree a thing, and it shall be established unto thee: and the light shall shine upon thy ways.
> When men are cast down, then thou shalt say, There is lifting up; and he shall save the humble person.
>
> Job 22:27-29

As a result, awesome breakthroughs took place in Job's life.

He had a larger family and greater wealth than ever before. At the end of his life, his state was 200% better than at first.

> After Job had prayed for his friends, the LORD made him prosperous again and gave him twice as much as he had before.
>
> Job 42:10 (NIV)

Once you discover the power of your declaration, you can have it not only for yourself but also for people around you.

The challenge we often face with financial declarations is that we do not fully believe in the power of our spoken words. We fail to believe God's Word regarding the creative ability of words. Because many factors affect our environment, we do not have the confidence, in the midst of chaos, to declare God's will. We do not believe that we will see His purposes accomplished as God speaks.

Declare the Vision and the Provision

Each year, in October, November, and December, I start praying regarding God's vision for the next calendar year. I ask to know the purpose in which I am to walk and the plan to implement it. Also, before the first of every year, I establish a vow in my heart for my "giving goal" during the next year. Then, I proclaim the purpose and vision God has revealed to me. Also, I decree the finances to be released, so I may accomplish God's objectives each year. For 20 years, I have done this.

Whenever I give to the Lord, I write on the offering envelopes my vision and giving-goal vow for that year. I remind Him, "God, this is my vow. I am fulfilling Your purpose in this earth. Now, fulfill the words that I have declared in the financial arena." It's interesting to see what happens throughout each year. Sometimes the amount of money God releases to me for giving is amazing! For example, in 1996 I underestimated how God would move financially, and I exceeded my vow by 250%! You might be wondering if I had any natural ways to make this happen. Absolutely not. How can this be? It is because the power of proclamation works.

It is possible to cross financial thresholds when you tie the money to God's purpose and prove that He can trust you. God is eager to release finances if He knows that when you receive them, you will give His part back to Him. The blessing of provision results when you:

- Align yourself with God's vision and purpose.
- Proclaim your vision and provision into being.
- Declare your vow and give to God.

Then, you will see the purpose and will of God accomplished in your life. Are you ready to step into supernatural breakthroughs? Remember, we have studied:

> But thou shalt remember the LORD thy God: for it is he that giveth thee power to get wealth, that he may establish his covenant which he sware unto thy fathers, as it is this day.
>
> Deuteronomy 8:18

Provision follows vision; it does not follow need. We will pursue our discussion on this topic in the next chapter. However, let me say this: Most people put their needs on their prayer lists. Instead, why not put your vision? As you pray, forecast the future. Take your vision before God, proclaim your provision, and declare your vow. Remember, your words bring life or death to your vision:

> Death and life are in the power of the tongue: and
> they that love it shall eat the fruit thereof.
>
> Proverbs 18:21

I am confident that the Church has not experienced a crashing
wave of increase because we are not in continuous alignment
with God's vision. I have experienced this in my life. For
example, in 1976 the gas company threatened to shut off the gas
to my trailer, because I did not have enough money to pay the
bill. However, year after year since then, my giving has exceeded
my 1976 gross income!

The Voice of Money

Do you realize that money has a voice? Have you ever
spoken to yourself about your financial situation? Most people
do mutter about money. Where do these ideas come from? You
must realize that you can hear thoughts from money! Then,
without recognizing it, you can find yourself speaking those
thoughts into existence. Remember, your words carry creative
power. By proclaiming the negative voice of money, you can
severely cripple your finances. Let me explain.

One day I was standing in line behind a man at a checkout
counter, when I noticed he was having difficulty paying for his
merchandise. Peering into his wallet, he appeared to be arguing
with himself about what he was seeing. I moved a little closer
to watch and listen.

Every credit card he looked at created a different grumbling
within the man. His attitude ranged from anger to fear and from
frustration to hopelessness. Surprisingly, he forecasted the
financial failure of his future children. As he continued leafing

through his billfold, he came to his pay stub. Now, he blurted out to himself hatred for his job and the desire that the ——— job would ———. He removed his cash and, after mumbling another self-destructive prophecy, he paid the cashier.

However, before leaving the store, he said to the clerk, "With all this, how can I ever afford to get married? My girlfriend just wants to settle down, get married, and start a family. I don't know how anybody can afford to be married, let alone have kids!" Looking at her wedding ring, he continued, "Do you have any kids?"

She replied, "Why do you think I'm behind this ——— register? You don't think I want to be here, do you? My husband and I just pass each other in the night between jobs."

"See, I'll be da—— if I'm going to live like this!" he cursed. "My kids will never know me. Well, I guess not until they want some of my money, too!" Holding his wallet in his clenched hand, he waved it at her as he walked off.

Then, it was my turn in line. As I approached the register, I asked, "Wow, what was his problem?"

She replied, "What do people expect from me? I only work here to try to make ends meet. It is no wonder that people end up being shot on their jobs. Just look at that guy! He is flipped out, and I have my own money problems!"

As I walked away from the counter, I looked into my own billfold, wondering, *Am I this frustrated, too?*

That night I taught at a financial freedom conference. My topic was *Tapping the Money Gap*, which I have since developed into a tape series. I explained that between the cost and sale price of an item, there is a gap called profit. Earlier in this book, we studied God's Word in Isaiah:

Thus saith the LORD, thy Redeemer, the Holy One of

Israel; I am the LORD thy God which *teacheth thee to profit,*
which leadeth thee by the way that thou shouldest go.

Isaiah 48:17

The thrust of my message that night was why do we spend most
of our money giving profit to others, when God promised to
teach *us* to profit?

At this meeting, I thought, *Let's see what happens to this
assembly of Christians when I ask them to take out their cash,
checkbooks, credit cards, wallets, purses, etc., and look at them.* As I
said these words, some people looked at me angrily. Fear came
over others. Some were astonished, and others obviously
thought, *Here we go. He is going to take an offering!* Immediately
the atmosphere became heavy. To lighten matters, I joked,
"Fear not! I'm not taking an offering!" Some giggled, others
sighed with relief, but some were still skeptical. The atmosphere
became a little lighter, but not very much.

I thought, *If this is how the Church responds before they even look
at their wallets, what will happen when they open them?* I had to
interrupt their anticipation of an offering or whatever they
expected, so I asked them to stand with only their cash, credit
cards, etc., in hand. However, I stated the condition that they
must hold all the finances they had with them. It took time for
some of them to comply. Others were obstinate. Apparently
they refused to do it! Over and over, I asked them to tell each
other, "He is not talking an offering! Just do what he says, and
don't fear!" Finally, they were all standing with their monies in
hand.

The second condition I set was that they had to look at me
and not at what was in their hands. Now, the stage was set. My
test was finally about to begin.

I then said, "Close your eyes, and release yourself from any

91

confusion or fear. In Jesus' Name! Now open your eyes, and look at your credit cards one by one, now your money, and now your checkbook. Okay, stop, and look at me!"

As each looked at me, I simply asked: "How many of you had thoughts that were fearful, frustrated, worrisome, or anxious? Now that you looked at your credit cards, checkbook, or cash, are you having thoughts that make you angry, accusing someone of something? You may even have had thoughts that forecast a negative picture about your future. Finally, maybe your mind immediately went to a negative thought. If any of these happened to you just now, raise your hand."

After these questions, about 80% of the people lifted their hands. Then, the other 20% raised their hands after I explained how to recognize a negative thought. Therefore, in my test, 100% had received a negative thought—in church!

You might be wondering what this is all about. Are you ready? Can you stand another new thought? Well, ready or not here it comes!

After they all acknowledged that they had received negative thoughts, I told them to turn in their Bibles to Ecclesiastes 10:19:

A feast is made for laughter, and wine maketh merry: *but money answereth all things.*

Ecclesiastes 10:19

Then I said to the people, "Now repeat after me, 'Money answers!' Say it again, 'Money answers!' Now ask yourself what does it answer?"

Of course, many replied, "All things." However, no one appeared to know what this meant.

I continued, explaining what had happened when they had looked at their money. In their thoughts, they had heard the answer that money was speaking back to them.

I know this might be a new thought, but when was the last time you had a new thought? Please continue reading, because this can change forever how you allow your money to answer you.

Yes, money had simply answered back to each person according to his own thoughts and the words he had previously spoken to his money. Money had not asked any questions, nor did its voice initiate any conversations. No, the Word of God says that money has an answer.

Then, I asked the people, "Do you like how your money talks to you? Do you allow everything to speak that way to you and do nothing about it?"

One by one, I could see the revelation dawn on some of them. They realized and thought, *Yes, the instant I looked at my money, I received negative thoughts.*

I also saw the doubt in some who still questioned me, so I asked them to turn to Genesis 2:16-17. We read the following:

> And the LORD God commanded the man, saying, Of every tree of the garden thou mayest freely eat:
> But of the tree of the knowledge of good and evil, thou shalt not eat of it: for in the day that thou eatest thereof thou shalt surely die.
>
> Genesis 2:16-17

Then I asked, "Did the forbidden tree produce apples, pears, or oranges?" Obviously not! I explained that it produced *knowledge*, which mankind could ingest! We know that the Fall of man occurred in the Garden of Eden when Adam and Eve ingested this knowledge. Suddenly they understood good and evil. However, God wanted them to avoid this knowledge, but why? One of His reasons was that He did not want mankind to experience negative thoughts.

You see, after they disobeyed God by eating of the forbidden tree, Adam and Eve began to experience the first negative thoughts:

> Then the eyes of both of them were opened, and they realized they were naked; so they sewed fig leaves together and made coverings for themselves.
>
> Then the man and his wife heard the sound of the LORD God as he was walking in the garden in the cool of the day, and they hid from the LORD God among the trees of the garden.
>
> But the LORD God called to the man, "Where are you?"
>
> He answered, "I heard you in the garden, and I was afraid because I was naked; so I hid."
>
> Genesis 3:7-10

Suddenly, Adam's and Eve's physical nakedness produced fear. What they saw and heard in their natural environment caused negative thoughts. Similarly, physical money can arouse negative thoughts in you, like it did for all the people at my financial meeting that night.

Now, since the Fall of man, it is common for us to receive thoughts from the enemy that come through our physical environment. Today, when some people get on a bridge, they experience the thought of jumping over the edge. Others see a river, and they feel like they are drowning. Still others step onto an elevator and sense they will fall; or they fly in a plane and think it will crash. These are phobias and fears that the Devil speaks to people through the physical realm. Money answers us in the same way, but not with an audible voice.

After explaining this at my meeting, I said, "Now, we must ask ourselves, 'Can I change the answer of my money?'" Now,

I had their attention.

Immediately, I reminded them of Jesus' Words in Mark 11:23:

> For verily I say unto you, That whosoever shall say unto this mountain, Be thou removed, and be thou cast into the sea; and shall not doubt in his heart, but shall believe that those things which he saith shall come to pass; he shall have whatsoever he saith.
>
> Mark 11:23

I continued, "Stand up. Now, speak to your money. Tell it how you want it to answer you from now on! In Jesus' Name! Did you get it? Yes, you speak. Then, your money will say, 'Yes, sir' or 'Yes, ma'am!' Now take out your money again, and get ready to tell it what kind of answers you want it to speak from now on!"

Then, I led them, saying, "Get focused, and speak with me to your money: 'In Jesus' Name, Money, you will never speak back to me like that again. I am your master, and you are my servant. I tell you where to go, and you go. I tell you when to come, and you come. From now on you will answer all things with, "Yes! I bless my master with abundance!" Now, Money, if I ever hear you answer again without respect and negatively, I will discard you and get some more! Then you will never have the privilege of serving me again!'"

Silence then filled the room. I could have heard a pin drop.

"Look at your money once more," I said. "Tell me if it speaks negatively to you again." There was a short silence. Then the meeting erupted with shouts of joy, clapping, and thanksgiving to God. The people had once again understood God's Word, acted on it, and saw the results.

Now, it is your turn. Take out your money, credit cards, and checkbook. Look at them. Then listen. Yes, you know what to do next.

Now pray this prayer with me:

> Father, I believe I am not simply existing on the earth. You have called me with a divine purpose and ordained me to inherit Your every promise. Now, I speak Your purpose and vision into being. I proclaim Your plan into existence. I know You will teach me to profit, and You will lead me in the way I should go.
>
> My presence is proof that You bless Your people. You have blessed me coming in and going out. I am the head and not the tail. Whatever I put my hand to prospers. I shout aloud, "The Lord takes pleasure in the prosperity of His servants! The Lord takes pleasure in the prosperity of *me*, His servant."
>
> I declare to You, Father, the vision that is in my heart, and I speak forth that it WILL come to pass. I speak the release of wealth, for it is Yours and will serve Your vision. When I receive it, Lord, I will sow into Your Kingdom's work again.
>
> Now, I speak to my money. In Jesus' Name, I command it to answer me with respect and without any back talk. I am a child of the Most High God. Money must serve me and the Prophetic Vision my God has called me to fulfill. From now on, I will not entertain any negative thoughts of the enemy through my money. Thank You, God, for giving authority to me to proclaim Your will in the earth today. In Jesus' name. Amen."

7
Release Vision-Driven Provision

Many people do not understand the next *Millionaire Mentality* principle, Provision, which we will discuss in this chapter. For years, I also labored under wrong thinking in this area, and my visions suffered from it. Now, I believe this simple revelation will revolutionize your finances as it did mine.

There Is No Provision without a Vision

First, let's consider the term *provision.* The prefix *pro* means "for or on behalf of." Provision, then, must be released on behalf of a vision to fulfill it. Now, if you do not have a vision, what are provisions for? You don't need them unless you have a vision!

You see, there are three motivations for wealth: Need, greed and vision.

Some people have such great needs that they strive for wealth, believing it will satisfy their emptiness. Others simply desire to be rich, because they are greedy. A lustful motivation to gain wealth drives both types of people. However, when they obtain their goal, sorrow comes with it. Their pain is directly related to the love of money, not the blessing of God.

Your Heavenly Father is not against your having wealth. However, He does not want wealth or the pursuit of it to control your life! Clearly, His Word warns against the love of money and the all-consuming motivation to acquire wealth.

But godliness with contentment is great gain.

For we brought nothing into the world, and we can take nothing out of it.

But if we have food and clothing, we will be content with that.

People who want to get rich fall into temptation and a trap and into many foolish and harmful desires that plunge men into ruin and destruction.

For the *love of money* is a root of all kinds of evil. Some people, eager for money, have wandered from the faith and pierced themselves with many griefs [*sorrows* (KJV)].

1 Timothy 6:6-10 (NIV)

On the other hand, some people receive visions from God. Instead of need or greed as their driving force, they desire to see God's vision fulfilled. They want to see what God can build. As these people move toward their visions, He blesses the work of their hands. With it comes no sorrow, according to Proverbs 10:22, which we studied earlier.

The great wealth that God desires to pour into your life to fulfill His vision far surpasses your current needs. In fact, frantically working simply to meet your needs is not even close to His best for you. He does not bless this kind of cursed motivation. Instead, God intends for wealth to follow you—not for you to follow wealth.

Jesus said signs follow believers:

And these signs shall follow them that believe; In my name shall they cast out devils; they shall speak with new tongues;

They shall take up serpents; and if they drink any deadly thing, it shall not hurt them; they shall lay hands on the sick, and they shall recover.

And they went forth, and preached every where, the Lord working with them, and confirming the word with signs following. Amen.

Mark 16:17-18, 20

Similarly, wealth will follow you when you obey God. It is a by-product of following your God-given vision. This is what I call vision-driven provision. Remember, God is your source. When you seek Him first, He adds everything else to you:

But seek ye first the kingdom of God, and his righteousness; *and all these things shall be added unto you.*

Matthew 6:33

This is a basic principle throughout the Bible.

Follow Biblical Examples of Vision-Driven Provision

The Old Covenant Scriptures contain many examples of supernatural provision from God. Let's examine some of these now, starting with briefly recalling our study of the Israelites, then moving to the lives of Abraham, Isaac, and Jacob.

The Israelites Needed to Pass God's Tests

Daily, God provided manna for the Israelites. Remember, they had to wander in the wilderness for 40 years, so they would learn that man does not live by bread alone but by every Word from God. The Israelites needed to realize they were not to live by material substance. Instead, God's Words and His visions were to be their focus. Only then would the provision come.

Israel had to see God differently. They needed to open their eyes to recognize that God Himself was their provision.

God Blessed *All* Nations through Abraham

Think again about Abraham. When his name was still Abram, he had a vision and purpose in his spirit. As we studied earlier, God told him:

> ..."Get out of your country,
> From your kindred
> And from your father's house,
> To a land that I will show you.
> I will make you a great nation;
> I will bless you
> And make your name great;
> And you shall be a blessing.
> I will bless those who bless you,
> And I will curse him who curses you;
> And in you all the families of the earth shall be blessed."
>
> Genesis 12:1-3 (NKJV)

God's purpose was to create from Abram a great nation that would bless all humanity.

In those days, no knowledge of God or Jehovah existed. In fact, Abram's father, Terah, worshipped pagan idols:

> And Joshua said unto all the people, Thus saith the LORD God of Israel, Your fathers dwelt on the other side of the flood in old time, even Terah, the father of Abraham, and the father of Nachor: and they served other gods.
>
> And I took your father Abraham from the other side of the flood, and led him throughout all the land of Canaan....
>
> Joshua 24:2-3

No one had told Abram about God, so God gave Abram a personal encounter with Himself. He made a new covenant with Abram and had to supply him with supernatural provision. Father God promised to Abram:

> ...Lift up now thine eyes, and look from the place where thou art northward, and southward, and eastward, and westward:
>
> For all the land which thou seest, to thee will I give it, and to thy seed for ever.
>
> And I will make thy seed as the dust of the earth: so that if a man can number the dust of the earth, then shall thy seed also be numbered.
>
> Arise, walk through the land in the length of it and in the breadth of it; for I will give it unto thee.
>
> Genesis 13:14 -17

Just think: God promised to give to Abram His gifts—something for which he did not work, strive, or qualify. Abram's only requirement was to believe that God would fulfill His promise. However, Abram had a difficult challenge. Already in old age, he and his wife were childless.

Then a shock came when Abram was 99 years old, and his wife, Sarai, was 90. God changed Abram's name to Abraham, which means father of many nations (Genesis 17:5). He changed Sarai's name to Sarah (Genesis 17:15), which means princess of many nations. Now, realize that God renamed them one year *before* their son, Isaac, was born (Genesis 17:21). What a Prophetic Vision this was!

How do you react to promises like these? Do you see God's vision or what limits you from receiving His promise? Do you respond, "Well, God, I hear what You are saying, but what about————?"

At first, Abraham challenged God about this vision. Through supernatural intervention, God had blessed him with cattle, silver, and gold (Genesis 13:2). God had created this wealth for him, and Abraham did not have to work for it. Yet, in effect he complained in Genesis 15:2-3, "God, You have given these financial blessings to me—and that's wonderful—but where is my child? How can I be the father of many nations when I have no son or blood heirs?"

How did God respond to Abraham? He simply reiterated the vision and promised to fulfill it:

> ..."Look now toward heaven, and count the stars if you are able to number them." And He said to him, "So shall your descendants be."
>
> And he [Abraham] believed in the Lord, and He accounted it to him for righteousness.
>
> Genesis 15:5-6 (NKJV)

Finally, Abraham believed in the vision. His heart had to connect to God to release Heaven's provision. If he, instead, had remained in the natural realm of life, Abraham would not have accomplished God's vision to become whom God had called him to be. He would not have had the faith, voice, and influence that we still recognize today. Without his spiritual encounters with God, Abraham would not have fulfilled God's purpose.

God had a vision for Abraham's life, and in every step He supplied the provision. Remember, Jesus Christ came through the lineage of Abraham. Think about it, God actually provided *through* Abraham for *all* humanity!

Isaac Discovered that Abundance Follows God's Promises

When Abraham died, he left nothing to his son, Isaac.

Abraham had experienced famine; and, in Genesis 26:1, the Bible declares that Isaac also lived in a land of terrible famine. Yet God promised to bless Isaac, saying:

> Sojourn in this land, and I will be with thee, and will bless thee; for unto thee, and unto thy seed, I will give all these countries, and I will perform the oath which I sware unto Abraham thy father;
> And I will make thy seed to multiply as the stars of heaven, and will give unto thy seed all these countries; and in thy seed shall all the nations of the earth be blessed.
> Genesis 26:3-4

Isaac chose not to act on the appearance of the famine but acted in faith on God's dream:

> Then Isaac sowed in that land, and received in the same year an hundredfold: and the LORD blessed him.
> And the man waxed great, and went forward, and grew until he became very great:
> For he had possession of flocks, and possession of herds, and great store of servants: and the Philistines envied him.
> Genesis 26:12-14

When he stepped into God's promises, Isaac stepped into abundance.

Jacob Understood that God's Blessings May Be Delayed, But Not Denied

Next, let's examine the life of Jacob, Abraham's grandson and Isaac's son. The book of Genesis describes Jacob as a nomad, wandering in the desert, without flocks and herds. He owned nothing or very little. Jacob's father, Isaac, sent him to find a wife in the home of his uncle, Laban. Along the way, God gave Jacob a dream and promised to him the same as He had to Abraham:

> And he dreamed, and behold a ladder set up on the earth, and the top of it reached to heaven: and behold the angels of God ascending and descending on it.
>
> And, behold, the LORD stood above it, and said, I am the LORD God of Abraham thy father, and the God of Isaac: the land whereon thou liest, to thee will I give it, and to thy seed;
>
> And thy seed shall be as the dust of the earth, and thou shalt spread abroad to the west, and to the east, and to the north, and to the south: and in thee and in thy seed shall all the families of the earth be blessed.
>
> Genesis 28:12-14

At the place of the vision, Jacob set up and anointed a pillar. He renamed the city Bethel, which means House of God.

> And Jacob vowed a vow, saying, If God will be with me, and will keep me in this way that I go, and will give me bread to eat, and raiment to put on,
>
> So that I come again to my father's house in peace; then shall the LORD be my God:
>
> And this stone, which I have set for a pillar, shall be God's house: and of all that thou shalt give me I will surely give the tenth unto thee.
>
> Genesis 28:20-22

Jacob continued his journey, arrived in Uncle Laban's

homeland, and fell in love with his cousin Rachel. After Jacob labored for seven years to marry Rachel, Laban deceived him. Instead, he gave Leah, Rachel's older sister, to Jacob in marriage. Then, only after agreeing to work another seven years, Jacob finally was able to marry Rachel. He continued working for Laban six more years. Yet, after these 20 years of labor, Jacob still owned nothing.

Now, we know that God gave the Scriptures to us for our instruction. From our studies, we have seen that no matter how long the delay, God will intervene and fulfill His promises. He had promised to bless Jacob with the blessings of Abraham, and no one could stop to it. Although the blessings were delayed, they were not denied.

During Jacob's 20 years of labor, Laban had deceived him repeatedly and failed to pay his wages fully. Therefore, Jacob asked Laban to send him away to his own country with his wives and children. However, Laban realized that God had blessed his life because Jacob had been there, so Laban asked Jacob to stay. He told Jacob to ask for anything he wanted.

> ...And Jacob said, Thou shalt not give me any thing: if thou wilt do this thing for me, I will again feed and keep thy flock.
>
> Genesis 30:31

As we will study later, Jacob's grandfather, Abraham, had replied similarly to the King of Sodom, lest the king should say, "I have made Abraham rich." Jacob continued, explaining his agreement with Laban:

> I will pass through all thy flock to day, removing from thence all the speckled and spotted cattle, and all

the brown cattle among the sheep, and the spotted and speckled among the goats: and of such shall be my hire.

So shall my righteousness answer for me in time to come, when it shall come for my hire before thy face: every one that is not speckled and spotted among the goats, and brown among the sheep, that shall be counted stolen with me.

And Laban said, Behold, I would it might be according to thy word.

Genesis 30:32-34

Laban probably was thinking, *This will be wonderful, because I have only a small number of speckled and spotted animals.*

The story continues. While Jacob fed the rest of Laban's flocks, he carved chunks in various places from the bark of rods, so they looked spotted and speckled. He then put them into the gutters of the watering troughs where the animals would see them when they came to drink and conceive.

Where did this idea come from? Jacob needed an answer, and God had given a dream to him. Here's how Jacob described it to Rachel and Leah:

"In breeding season I once had a dream in which I looked up and saw that the male goats mating with the flock were streaked, speckled or spotted.

The angel of God said to me in the dream, 'Jacob.' I answered, 'Here I am.'

And he said, 'Look up and see that all the male goats mating with the flock are streaked, speckled or spotted, for I have seen all that Laban has been doing to you.

I am the God of Bethel, where you anointed a pillar and where you made a vow to me. Now leave this land at once and go back to your native land.'"

Genesis 31:10-13 (NIV)

Here, we see that God had told Jacob He would change the natural order of the animals' mating habits!

> And the flocks conceived before the rods, and brought forth cattle ringstreaked, speckled, and spotted.
> And Jacob did separate the lambs, and set the faces of the flocks toward the ringstreaked, and all the brown in the flock of Laban; and he put his own flocks by themselves, and put them not unto Laban's cattle.

Genesis 30:39-40

Jacob had put the vision, which God had given to him, constantly before the flocks' eyes. In this way, nothing would pollute the blessing of God's provision for him.

> And it came to pass, whensoever the stronger cattle did conceive, that Jacob laid the rods before the eyes of the cattle in the gutters, that they might conceive among the rods.
> But when the cattle were feeble, he put them not in: so the feebler were Laban's, and the stronger Jacob's.
> And the man increased exceedingly, and had much cattle, and maidservants, and menservants, and camels, and asses.

Genesis 30:41-43

Where did this increase come from? Jacob must have had such a multiplication of livestock that he had enough to sell and hire many servants. You see, Jacob trusted more in the provision for the vision, which God had given to him, than he did in the payment of wages due him after working 20 years for Laban! He trusted more in God's blessing than in his job of 20 years!

Now, Laban and his sons were unhappy because of Jacob's prosperity. God then spoke to Jacob, commanding him:

> ...Return unto the land of thy fathers, and to thy kindred; and I will be with thee.
>
> And Jacob sent and called Rachel and Leah to the field unto his flock,
>
> And said unto them, I see your father's countenance, that it is not toward me as before; but the God of my father hath been with me.
>
> Genesis 31:3-5

God released provision for the visions of each of these men: Abraham, Isaac, and Jacob. Also, remember, earlier we examined Joseph's life and found that God's dream in his heart exalted him and brought great wealth. Now, recall that Joseph was Jacob's son, so here we have four generations of dreamers! God fulfilled His promises to each of them, and they overflowed with financial blessings. Today, you and I should expect no less.

Do Not Take Any Shortcuts

In this book, we have plainly established that it is God's will for you to prosper. However, there are no shortcuts to God's blessings.

The Bible explains in Genesis 16 that Abraham and Sarah at first tried to speed God's dream through a carnal plan. They decided to have Abraham lie with their maidservant Hagar. The child she then bore, Ishmael, became Abraham's enemy and the forefather of today's Arabs, who still hate Israel. Additionally, if Abraham had stopped there, he would have short-circuited God's plan for the lineage of Jesus Christ!

What if Jacob had taken an easier way and had eloped with Rachel, instead of staying 20 years with Laban? He would not have received the flocks and extraordinary wealth God had planned for him. Nor would he have had Leah also as his wife, so he could bear the twelve tribes of Israel.

What if Joseph had decided to accept Potiphar's wife's invitation to sleep with her? (See Genesis 39-41.) What if he had thought he would find favor in her eyes and receive blessings through her? He would not have had the opportunity to interpret Pharaoh's dreams and rise to power in Egypt. Nor would he have held the position to provide for his father and brothers in their famine.

You see, shortcuts are not short in the long run!

Abraham, Isaac, Jacob, and Joseph patiently weathered their trials in integrity with faith and obedience. Likewise, we must follow God's dream, no matter how long or where it takes us. As God is true, He will not prosper you through violating His own Word by unethical, illegal, immoral or other ungodly activities. Nor does He bless haste in the pursuit of wealth.

In fact, God may allow some people to experience lengthy tests of character, such as He did with Abraham, Isaac, Jacob, and Joseph. Eventually, however, God provided them supernatural provision and wealth, and He will do the same for you. With long-suffering, they overcame all the obstacles to achieve their dreams. Few people desire long-suffering. However, none live above the laws of God's Word. If we want to achieve our dreams, we must patiently endure His tests with obedience and faith. Even after landing in financial ruin or bankruptcy, many have bounced back to the pinnacle of success.

God can do *anything* through you when you follow Him!

Resolve in your heart that nothing on earth that can defeat you. Jesus has made you more than a conqueror! Take every decision and align it with the Word of God. If God is not in agreement with an action, then neither are you! Press in beyond the natural limits that turn away the weak and faltering. Hold fast to the truth. Then, watch God prove His every Word!

> And we desire that every one of you do show the same diligence to the full assurance of hope unto the end:
> That ye be not slothful, but followers of them who through faith and patience inherit the promises.
> Hebrews 6:11-12

This earth and everything in it is one of your promises!

Take charge and seize every day as the last one you have. Live, knowing that God will fulfill His dream in you.

Do Not Settle for Leftovers

It is interesting to study the lives of Abraham, Isaac, Jacob, and Joseph. We find that each generation, from Abraham to Joseph, lost everything. The leftovers of God's promises did not pass from one generation to the next. Without help from forebears, each had to start over to seize his own promises from God. They had to begin from zero to move into abundance. To receive divine inheritances, each had a personal encounter with God and came to know Him. This activated God's promises, which then manifested in their lives.

Many people today try to live on the revelation of someone else's experience with God. They see God's provision for others and hope to receive the overflow. However, the runoff from someone else's experience with God is not enough. You must have your own encounter with Him.

Also, many believe that old, inherited wealth is the way to riches, but biblically this is not true. You see, it does not matter whether your forefathers touched God or if you received your rightful inheritance from a blessed person. It only matters whether you touch the dream realm of God yourself and receive His provision for your vision. If you have fully embraced in your heart God's purpose, then His very Words already have commanded the revenue to release as your provision. The blessing of "from zero to abundance" can be yours.

We must realize that we have a better covenant than Abraham, Isaac, and Jacob had. Jesus built ours upon better promises. Therefore, we should be seeing at least the beginning stages of God's promises. We should be having "speckled-and-spotted experiences" and not be on the payroll of someone else's value system. While there is nothing wrong with working for people, we should not let any job corrupt our beliefs or become our source of revenue. This is not God's plan for us. You see, wealth from God is created, not earned.

The Land of the Present and the Land of the Promise

One of the keys to releasing God's provision is what I call moving from the land of the present into the land of the promise. Abraham, Isaac, Jacob, and Joseph each stepped from his natural circumstances in the land of the present into the land of God's promises. As a result, they all walked into abundance.

Let's revisit Abraham's life for a few moments. He did not live in the land of his present ownership but in the land of God's promise.

> By faith Abraham, when he was called to go out into
> a place which he should after receive for an inheritance,
> obeyed; and he went out, not knowing whither he went.
> *By faith he sojourned in the land of promise,* as in a
> strange country, dwelling in tabernacles with Isaac and
> Jacob, the heirs with him of the same promise.
>
> Hebrews 11:8-9

Most people do not know how to live in the land of promise,
because it is not immediately within reach. They would prefer
to live in the land of ownership—what they have now. Usually,
man chooses to live in and settle for that which is immediately
present instead of God's promises. These are very different
places. You see, if you live only in what you have now, you will
never arrive where you could be. Your present and God's
promise are two entirely different lands. You must live beyond
the land of the present to step into the land of the promise.

By faith, Abraham lived "in the land of promise, as in a
strange country." The land of promise is an unusual place. You
can only step into it when you leave the arena of natural
limitations.

Now, when Abraham journeyed into the land of promise,
what did he look for?

> For he looked for a city which hath foundations,
> whose builder and maker is God.
>
> Hebrews 11:10

He searched for a city with foundations, which God had
built. You see, Abraham lived in tents for a reason. It was
because he refused his hands to interfere with God's work of
building a nation. From the beginning of his journey, Abraham
willingly lived in temporary housing until God finished His

work permanently.

In effect, Abraham obediently said: "I am a sojourner in a strange land, but I am looking for what God has promised will be mine. Until I see it, I will not settle for anything less. The God, who has spoken it, will perform it."

You see, God did not design your present to perform. He only designed His promise to perform. If you worked at a job from now until you die, would you spend everything and have nothing of any significance at the end? Many people live and die, never touching the purpose or the provision of God. If you settle only for a life in the apparent present, you will never live in the promise. You simply will not have enough money, time, or energy. You will lack the insight, foresight, and wisdom to handle God's plan for your life.

In the New Testament, the Apostle Paul stood on these truths:

> For our light affliction, which is but for a moment, worketh for us a far more exceeding and eternal weight of glory;
> While we look not at the things which are seen, but at the things which are not seen: for the things which are seen are temporal; but the things which are not seen are eternal.
>
> 2 Corinthians 4:17

You must operate in life on the basis of God's promises. When you live the vision and the vision lives in you, then provision can start to flow to you. Remember, provision is for the vision.

God's Purpose and Promise Always Release Provision

This is how Abraham, Isaac, Jacob, and Joseph not only

survived their challenges but also accomplished the great visions God had designed for them and their descendants.

How did Abraham start? He left a pagan worshipper's household when God spoke to him and eventually became a wealthy man, known as the father of our faith.

Think about Isaac. He faced a terrible famine. Yet after God spoke to him, he received a hundredfold harvest with flocks, herds, and many servants.

Jacob began as a vagabond in the desert, wandering, owning nothing, and leading no one. After God gave a dream to him, Jacob escaped Laban's abuse, taking with him great wealth, wives, children, many servants, and a multitude of speckled and spotted animals.

God's dream in Joseph's heart catapulted him from a prison to the palace and from a slave to the ruler of Egypt, second only to Pharaoh.

Let these testimonies bring hope to you. Realize that God's vision brings with it His provision. Sowing dream seeds causes everything to move on your behalf. You see, it is your dream—not the provision—that launches you on the journey to fulfillment.

When I was in business, I had a destructive mindset at first. I thought that if I could earn enough money in business, then I could be successful in ministry. If I had the provision, then I would have the vision. However, I discovered that I had it backwards, and the Heavens were like brass. Finally, God broke through to my spirit, saying, "You will not have enough money in the present to do what I say. You will only have it in the land of promise."

In the natural realm, the concepts God had spoken to me were financially unbelievable. Then, only three people attended my church, and we met in my living room. However, I had a vision for a choir, a band, a worship team, Bible schools covering the world, several thousand people worshipping God, and 1,000 full-time missionaries on the mission field!

God showed me that having nothing in the present does not influence what I have in the land of promise. You see, you and I do not need anything in the present. We only need the land of promise. Abraham, Isaac, Jacob, and Joseph came from nothing into the land of promise. They followed the Words God had spoken to them. Remember, the answers for everything we need are in the voice of God. In the vision, which God speaks to us, is the provision.

What prophetic Words has God said about your life? Are you following them? What vision is dawning inside you? As God had dreams for Abraham, Isaac, Jacob, and Joseph, He has a one for you, too. You may say, "No, I don't have an overriding vision." Well, if you are Christian, you do have the Holy Spirit within you. He knew you before you were born, and He understands the purpose of your existence. Your reason for living is no secret to the Holy Spirit. He knows the end before the beginning. Because He purposed it, who can annul it?

Listen to Him. What is the Spirit of God speaking to you from Heaven? What has He said about your future? Always remember, God fights for your vision, if it is from Him. He battles for His purpose. The Spirit of God will reveal it to you and accomplish the vision through you.

You can have the heavenly provision you need. Simply step over the threshold into it by obeying God. Are you willing, like Jacob, to carve something as simple as a branch and throw it into a trough, proclaiming, "Earth, I decree the dream of God to manifest!"? This is radical thinking compared to today's average workaday mindset. However, this is a different economy—God's heavenly economy!

Dreams cost nothing to receive, but most of us are afraid to have one because we fear failure. Until you live the vision and the vision lives in you, provision will not come. It cannot arrive, because it lacks a vision to attach itself to. Discover His dream for you. Begin to speak to it. Then, step out from the land of the present into the land of the promise!

It Starts with Your Identity in God

God told Abraham, Isaac, and Jacob that He would bless all the families of the earth through their seed. As we discussed earlier, we know that Jesus came from their lineage. What is the purpose of *your* existence? Jesus said that in Christ you are the light of the world, and through you (and other Christians) the world becomes saved. The lineage of Jesus Christ continues to bless all the people on earth through His followers.

Ye are the light of the world. A city that is set on an hill cannot be hid.

Neither do men light a candle, and put it under a bushel, but on a candlestick; and it giveth light unto all that are in the house.

Let your light so shine before men, that they may see your good works, and glorify your Father which is in heaven.

Matthew 5:14-16

As believers in Christ, we live the words of Paul and Barnabas:

For so hath the Lord commanded us, saying, I have set thee to be a light of the Gentiles, that thou shouldest be for salvation unto the ends of the earth.

Acts 13:47

The most meaningful matter on the face of this earth is eternal life. Everything else we do outside the purposes of God is wood, hay, and stubble, which will be destroyed and burned. Paul wrote:

> By the grace God has given me, I laid a foundation as an expert builder, and someone else is building on it. But each one should be careful how he builds.
>
> For no one can lay any foundation other than the one already laid, which is Jesus Christ.
>
> If any man builds on this foundation using gold, silver, costly stones, wood, hay or straw [stubble],
>
> his work will be shown for what it is, because the Day will bring it to light. It will be revealed with fire, and the fire will test the quality of each man's work.
>
> If what he has built survives, he will receive his reward.
>
> If it is burned up, he will suffer loss; he himself will be saved, but only as one escaping through the flames.
>
> 1 Corinthians 3:10-15 (NIV)

Nothing anyone does—no matter how noble and wonderful it might be—has any eternal reward to it except what one purposes in God.

Our God-given dreams reflect our significance and His ordained purpose for our lives. Realize that your purpose and identity are in God. The God of Abraham, Isaac, Jacob, and Joseph is *your* God, too, and He has not changed. The same God who brought these men of faith through life-threatening tribulations also will deliver you. The same God who provided for them will provide for you. When you allow God and His vision to become your focus, you can soar beyond all economic, educational, social, ethnic, and gender limitations, plus any other kind of obstacle.

Let the Dream Have You

Everything Abraham, Isaac, Jacob, and Joseph put their hands to prospered. What was the secret of their success? They were dream-driven! Throughout their lives, the dream carried them. God's visions for their lives had provision tied to them.

I titled this book *Millionaire Mentality*, but actually I am writing about Dream Mentality. I used the word *millionaire* to help you realize that this mentality has great value attached to it. If I had labeled it *Dream Mentality*, you might have said, "Well, I have had dreams before." However, have you really had *God's* dreams, and have His dreams had you? Until His dream has you, you don't have His dream.

Today many of us in the Body of Christ struggle to work our dreams using our own strength. Instead, we should yield to God's dreams and *His* strength. If we live in the limitless arena of God's Words and promises, we will walk in His limitless provision. Instead of looking forward, however, we look backward into the present, saying, "This isn't working. It's not happening. I might as well put a stop to this dream."

No! The dream that captures your heart is your deliverance. Your vision causes you to soar above the obstacles of mere humanity and everyday life. It's the dream that paves the way for your breakthrough. Abraham, Isaac, Jacob, and Joseph all had the opportunity to say, "This isn't working. It's not happening. I might as well put a stop to this dream." They had nothing at the inception of their dreams, and *you* don't need anything either. You only need the dream. Your provision is in the vision!

God Told Me to Live the Dream

As my wife, Faye, and I worked through our divorce and remarriage in 1975, I prayed in the Holy Spirit one day and God gave a vision to me. I saw fields of people—hundreds of thousands—come to Jesus. Then, He spoke to me, saying, "I have called you to reap the fields of the world."

At that time, my wife was suing me in divorce court. I told God, "You have one big problem." I had recently read the Scripture, which says:

> (For if a man know not how to rule his own house,
> how shall he take care of the church of God?)
> 1 Timothy 3:5

God answered me, saying, "If you will live the dream I have given to you, I will run your household!"

"That's a deal," I quickly responded, "because what I'm doing isn't working at all." I had done everything I knew to save my marriage, and nothing had worked.

The truth is the dream from God delivered our home and reconciled our marriage. When we remarried, I told Faye, "Do you realize that we are not remarrying for one another? We are remarrying for the fields of the world where God will touch His people." You see, marriage was a provision for the dream. The dream became our driving force. It was our call to His purpose.

Have you ever seen someone face miserable circumstances when he engaged in God's vision for his life? Then did he drop the dream, because his present became too frustrating? Did you watch as he lost his joy, momentum, motivation, and finances? Why did he lose almost everything of value? It was because anything outside his dream would not work for him.

Again, we must understand that man does not live by bread alone but by every Word that proceeds from the mouth of God. Live by what He says. Let His dream drive you. If you trust in your arm of the flesh—what *you* can do—the Bible says you are cursed. However, if your trust is in God, He will bless you:

> Thus saith the LORD; Cursed be the man that trusteth in man, and maketh flesh his arm, and whose heart departeth from the LORD.
> For he shall be like the heath in the desert, and shall not see when good cometh; but shall inhabit the parched places in the wilderness, in a salt land and not inhabited.
> Blessed is the man that trusteth in the LORD, and whose hope the LORD is.
> For he shall be as a tree planted by the waters, and that spreadeth out her roots by the river, and shall not see when heat cometh, but her leaf shall be green; and shall not be careful in the year of drought, neither shall cease from yielding fruit.
>
> Jeremiah 17:5-8

You will be like the godly man in Psalm 1. New life will start growing and blossoming around you:

> But his delight is in the law of the LORD; and in his law doth he meditate day and night.
> And he shall be like a tree planted by the rivers of water, that bringeth forth his fruit in his season; his leaf also shall not wither; and whatsoever he doeth shall prosper.
>
> Psalm 1:2-3

Even a Gentile King Helped Fulfill Nehemiah's Vision

Are you ready to allow the dream to drive your provision? Nehemiah was ready. Let's look at his dream now. This is a touching story about the Holy Spirit's infiltration in His people's lives to restore their vision and purpose. God inseminated the heart of Nehemiah with a dream to rebuild Jerusalem's walls, which Israel's enemies had destroyed in previous years.

Nehemiah, whose name means "Comfort of Jehovah," was the Jewish captive of a Gentile king named Artaxerxes. He held the trusted position of the king's personal cupbearer, which indicates his strong character and integrity. However, his dream moved him beyond his temporal environment and responsibilities:

> The words of Nehemiah the son of Hachaliah.
>
> It came to pass in the month of Chislev, in the twentieth year, as I was in Shushan the citadel,
>
> that Hanani one of my brethren came with men from Judah; and I asked them concerning the Jews who had escaped, who had survived the captivity, and concerning Jerusalem.
>
> And they said to me, "The survivors who are left from the captivity in the province are there in great distress and reproach. The wall of Jerusalem is also broken down, and its gates are burned with fire."
>
> So it was, when I heard these words, that I sat down and wept, and mourned for many days; I was fasting and praying before the God of heaven.
>
> Nehemiah 1:1-4 (NKJV)

Sometimes dreams affect you. You start noticing the chasms, social ills, pain, destruction, and injustices in your environment. What you see often grips your heart and moves you to tears. Take note when this happens to you, because these are the earmarks of God's vision within you. As you read the remaining portion of this story, think about what grips your heart and moves you to tears.

This is what happened to Nehemiah. Next, he recounted His prayer to God:

> ... "I pray, LORD God of heaven, O great and awesome God, You who keep Your covenant and mercy with those who love You and observe Your commandments,
>
> "please let Your ear be attentive and Your eyes open, that You may hear the prayer of Your servant which I pray before You now, day and night, for the children of Israel Your servants, and confess the sins of the children of Israel which we have sinned against You. Both my father's house and I have sinned.
>
> "We have acted very corruptly against You, and have not kept the commandments, the statutes, nor the ordinances which You commanded Your servant Moses."
>
> Nehemiah 1:5-7 (NKJV)

One day when Nehemiah was fulfilling his role as cupbearer, King Artaxerxes saw his unusual countenance and asked Nehemiah:

> ... "Why is your face sad, since you are not sick? This is nothing but sorrow of heart." Then I became dreadfully afraid,
>
> and said to the king, "May the king live forever! Why should my face not be sad, when the city, the place of my fathers' tombs, lies waste, and its gates are burned with fire?"
>
> Then the king said to me, "What do you request?" So I prayed to the God of heaven.
>
> And I said to the king, "If it pleases the king, and if your servant has found favor in your sight, I ask that you send me to Judah, to the city of my fathers' tombs, that

I may rebuild it."

So the king said to me (the queen also sitting beside him), "How long will your journey be? And when will you return?" So it pleased the king to send me; and I set him a time.

Furthermore I said to the king, "If it pleases the king, let letters be given to me for the governors of the region beyond the River, that they must permit me to pass through till I come to Judah,

"and a letter to Asaph the keeper of the king's forest, that he must give me timber to make beams for the gates of the citadel which pertains to the temple, for the city wall, and for the house that I will occupy." And the king granted them to me according to the good hand of my God upon me.

Nehemiah 2:2-8 (NKJV)

Provision came when the vision penetrated Nehemiah's spirit. In effect, he said to the Gentile king, "I have a vision, and I want you to do something about it." What did the king do? He gave Nehemiah all the materials necessary to finish the entire job of building the wall around Jerusalem. When you obey God and let His dream drive you, your provision can come from the most unlikely places.

Like Zechariah, You Will Receive Grace from God

The last story I want to share in this chapter is that of another builder, Zerubbabel. God gave to him the dream of rebuilding the temple of Jerusalem. The Prophet Zechariah shared the Word from God:

"This is the word of the Lord to Zerubbabel:
'Not by might nor by power, but by My Spirit,'

Says the LORD of hosts.
'Who are you, O great mountain?
Before Zerubbabel you shall become a plain!
And he shall bring forth the capstone with shouts of
    "Grace, grace to it."'"

Zechariah 4:6-7 (NKJV)

Would Zerubbabel have to struggle to achieve his goal? Oh, no! Here, the Spirit of God promised to accomplish the vision with shouts of grace!

What is grace? Where does it come from, and how does it work? How can you know when you are operating in it? Some have shared that grace is *"God's Riches At Christ's Expense."* I recognize grace intervening in my life when the dream and vision are far beyond my human ability, and God shows up to do it Himself! I am only able to shout with Him, because I realize that I could not have made it happen in my strength.

Let's continue our study on how the Holy Spirit worked with Zerubbabel, according to the Prophet Zechariah:

…"The hands of Zerubbabel
Have laid the foundation of this temple;
His hands shall also finish it.
Then you will know that the Lord of hosts has sent
    Me to you.
For who has despised the day of small things?
For these seven [eyes of the Lord] rejoice to see
The plumb line in the hand of Zerubbabel.
They are the eyes of the Lord,
Which scan to and fro throughout the whole earth."

Zechariah 4:8-10 (NKJV)

Zerubbabel ran with God's vision to restore Solomon's temple. Dare I say that if you can tap into God's desires, you will never know a day of loss or lack in your life? You will accomplish it not by your might or power, but by His Spirit. It will be by His grace, not by the work of man's flesh or mind. Step over the threshold right now, and proclaim:

I am a dream-driven believer. The dream seeds, which God has sown within my spirit, literally are causing provision to follow me!

Pray this with me now as we close this chapter on Provision:

God, I pray that I would become dream-led. Move me with Your Prophetic Vision and purpose like You did for Nehemiah. Release me from the influences of anything that would bind and restrain. Mind of God, I yield to You and submit to Your dreams and visions. I believe that Your vision will release provision in my life. Like Abraham, Isaac, Jacob, and Joseph, I let You multiply me.

Like Zerubbabel, I build Your vision with a capstone of grace. For I know that the vision is accomplished not by might nor by power, but by Your Spirit. Hallelujah! I cry "grace" to it. In Jesus' Name. Amen.

8
Tap into Heaven's Wealth

Now, we have seen that your dreams, perspective, actions, and words are of utmost significance if you are to engage God's provision in your life. This last chapter will assist you in activating several additional secrets to help you tap into Heaven's wealth.

Unlock Financial Results

In previous chapters, we examined Abraham's relationship with God. In our study, we saw that he obeyed, received God's promise when Sarah conceived and bore Isaac, and became extremely wealthy. Abraham knew God as his provider:

> And the king of Sodom said unto Abram, Give me the persons, and take the goods to thyself.
> And Abram said to the king of Sodom, I have lift up mine hand unto the LORD, the most high God, the possessor of heaven and earth,
> That I will not take from a thread even to a shoelatchet, and that I will not take any thing that is thine, lest thou shouldest say, I have made Abram rich.
>
> Genesis 14:21-23

Remember, Abraham's grandson, Jacob, had said something similar to Laban. No one would be able to say that Laban had made Jacob rich—only God could have performed such a miracle.

We must grasp how Abraham unlocked the financial results he experienced. Initially, we will examine four keys Abraham knew. The first key is an absolute resolve that God created everything in existence. Secondly, believe that God retains ownership of the heavens and earth and everything in them. The third key is one of action: Abraham gave to God one-tenth of all he had and received. The fourth key is Abraham knew how to withdraw from God's heavenly bank account. This study will reveal awesome truths, which few have fully experienced.

1. God Created Everything in Existence

We studied in a previous chapter that the first chapter of Genesis opens our eyes to the creative power of God's spoken Word. The very Words from God's mouth were the things created. This truth alone reveals more to you may than you think.

If we would only apply this truth to our personal lives, we would live unlimited. For example, let's say that during a quiet one-on-one prayer time, you hear God speak to your spirit that He is fully supplying all your needs according to Philippians 4:19:

> But my God shall supply all your need according to his riches in glory by Christ Jesus.
>
> Philippians 4:19

This Word brings confidence and support, because you know that you cannot provide for yourself as God can. However, most people stop right there. Do not stop! God has purposed that *Rhema* Word to manifest with more than having your needs met. Yes, "according to His riches in glory" means much more than your supply. It is not according to your need but according to His riches! Pray and ask your Heavenly Father to reveal this truth to you. Remember the Words of Jesus:

> Then said Jesus to those Jews which believed on him,
> *If ye continue in my word,* then are ye my disciples indeed;
> And *ye shall know the truth, and the truth shall make you free.*
>
> John 8:31-32

When we focus on an area of the Scripture by reading, believing, and speaking it to ourselves over and over, we will receive revelation knowledge from the Lord. Ultimately, the manifestation of the Word will come.

2. God Retains Ownership of the Heavens and Earth and Everything in Them

With this primary thought in mind, we must conclude that we are only stewards and not owners. Abraham had a clear understanding of this truth. After he won a battle against those who stole Lot's (his nephew) wives, children, and goods he refused to identify with a human reward system:

> And he brought back all the goods, and also brought again his brother Lot, and his goods, and the women also, and the people.
> And the king of Sodom went out to meet him after his return from the slaughter of Chedorlaomer, and of the kings that were with him, at the valley of Shaveh, which is the king's dale.
> And the king of Sodom said unto Abram, Give me the persons, and take the goods to thyself.
> And Abram said to the king of Sodom, *I have lift up*

mine hand unto the LORD, the most high God, the possessor of heaven and earth,

That I will not take from a thread even to a shoelatchet, and that *I will not take any thing that is thine, lest thou shouldest say, I have made Abram rich:*

Save only that which the young men have eaten, and the portion of the men which went with me, Aner, Eshcol, and Mamre; let them take their portion.

Genesis 14:16-17, 21-24

Here, we see that Abraham clearly knew he would become very wealthy. This man saw only one source! Everything He had would come from God.

3. Give to God One-Tenth of All You Have and Receive from All Revenue Sources

This key is absolutely critical. It is not only a physical deed but also an act of one's heart.

First, let's separate the difference between tithes and offerings. Simply put, the *tithe* (which means a tenth or ten percent) is the first one-tenth of all your revenue. Notice that it is the *first* one-tenth. When you pay your tithes, it must be from your firstfruits. In the Old Testament, the firstfruits were the first part of the harvest. Your tithes must not come from leftovers.

On the other hand, offerings are anything you give above and beyond the first one-tenth. Here, I will not dwell extensively on the differences; many other authors have excellent books on this topic.

Paying tithes began before the Law of Moses and continued through Abraham's life. We studied earlier that Abraham's grandson Jacob also vowed to tithe in Genesis 28:22. Today, God's Word still commands us to tithe.

Look at the following account of Abraham having a covenant meal with Melchizedek. Here, they shared an experience of communion as they enjoyed a singleness of heart. Abraham saw a true connection to God through giving. This occurred after Abraham returned from defeating King Chedorlaomer of Elam and the other kings aligned with him.

> And Melchizedek king of Salem brought forth bread and wine: and he was the priest of the most high God.
>
> And he blessed him, and said, Blessed be Abram of the most high God, possessor of heaven and earth:
>
> And blessed be the most high God, which hath delivered thine enemies into thy hand. *And he gave him tithes of all.*
>
> Genesis 14:18-20

Now, Melchizedek was not like any other man, but like the Son of God Himself. In fact, in Hebrews 7:8, the Bible states that on earth men who die receive your tithes, but God also receives them in Heaven:

> For this Melchizedek, king of Salem, priest of the most high God, who met Abraham returning from the slaughter of the kings, and blessed him;
>
> To whom also Abraham gave a tenth part of all; first being by interpretation King of righteousness, and after that also King of Salem, which is, King of peace;
>
> Without father, without mother, without descent, having neither beginning of days, nor end of life; but made like unto the Son of God; abideth a priest continually.
>
> Now consider how great this man was, unto whom

even the patriarch Abraham gave the tenth of the spoils.

And *here men that die receive tithes;* but *there he receiveth them, of whom it is witnessed that he liveth.*

And as I may so say, Levi also, who receiveth tithes, payed tithes in Abraham.

Hebrews 7:1-4, 8-9

Realize that you pay your tithes directly to God Himself.

Today, many believers dispute the practice of tithing. That is very unfortunate, because God's Word declares that we must honor Him with the first tenth of everything (before paying any bills, etc.). Otherwise, the entire amount of money is cursed. It is far better to have a blessed 90% than a cursed 100%. Look with me into the book of Malachi:

> Will a man rob God? Yet ye have robbed me. But ye say, Wherein have we robbed thee? In tithes and offerings.
>
> *Ye are cursed with a curse: for ye have robbed me,* even this whole nation.
>
> Bring ye all the tithes into the storehouse, that there may be meat in mine house, and prove me now herewith, saith the LORD of hosts, if I will not open you the windows of heaven, and pour you out a blessing, that there shall not be room enough to receive it.
>
> And I will rebuke the devourer for your sakes, and he shall not destroy the fruits of your ground; neither shall your vine cast her fruit before the time in the field, saith the LORD of hosts.
>
> And all nations shall call you blessed: for ye shall be a delightsome land, saith the LORD of hosts.

Malachi 3:8-12

You must understand the phrase "that there may be meat in

mine house" in light of the New Testament. Jesus explained God's definition:

> Jesus saith unto them, My meat is to do the will of him that sent me, and to finish his work.
>
> John 4:34

Therefore, when you give your tithes and offerings it is so the Church can do the will of God on earth.

Jesus amplified this principle by stating:

> For where your treasure is, there will your heart be also.
>
> Matthew 6:21

Your heart and your treasure tie closely together. Jesus also explained that without honoring God with the heart attitude and actions of giving, you will trust something else as your source of financial sustenance. Many live bound and cursed, because they trust their skills, education, retirement, or jobs for their livelihood. Proud that they are "self-made" men, some trust their savings, stocks, bonds, or even themselves.

Our Lord continued in this passage:

> For where your treasure is, there will your heart be also.
>
> The light of the body is the eye: if therefore thine eye be single, thy whole body shall be full of light.
>
> But if thine eye be evil (or covetous), thy whole body shall be full of darkness. If therefore the light that is in thee be darkness, how great is that darkness!
>
> *No man can serve two masters: for either he will hate the one, and love the other; or else he will hold to the one, and*

despise the other. Ye cannot serve God and mammon.
Matthew 6:21-24

Here, Jesus warned us not to become caught in the world's systems of false security, because in the world everything vanishes with the using. It is all right to have a high-paying job, savings, retirement accounts, and awesome wealth. However, you must not put your trust in these.

In the above passage, Jesus said that trusting in the security or provision of something other than God was trusting in the master called "mammon." In that era, Mammon was the well-known provision god of three pagan empires: Babylon, Assyria, and Egypt. These three kingdoms worshipped Mammon for support and revenue like we today trust in retirement accounts so we will not have to work. Well, obviously the false god of Mammon actually provided no provisions, neither do our retirement accounts.

You might be thinking, *No, my retirement assets are safe. I have invested them in low-risk mutual funds and AAA-rated bonds. I'll be able to take it easy when it's time to retire.* On this note, Jesus made some of the most profound statements in the Word about your financial security on the earth:

Lay not up for yourselves treasures upon earth, where moth and rust doth corrupt, and where thieves break through and steal:

But lay up for yourselves treasures in heaven, where neither moth nor rust doth corrupt, and where thieves do not break through nor steal.
Matthew 6:19-20

Jesus said it. That settles it. When we store up wealth on

earth, it is not safe. Thieves can steal it, and it can wither away in various ways. For example, what would happen to our finances if the stock market crashed? God alone is our only security.

With Jesus' bold and revealing statement that our earthly treasures can be stolen, you may question what is *Millionaire Mentality* all about? You need to use money here on earth, so how can you *not* store it on earth? If you store it in Heaven, how can you use it on earth? This paradox has hindered man for 2,000 years. How does it work?

4. Learn to Withdraw from God's Heavenly Bank Account

In the next few paragraphs, I will share key secrets, which I have discovered about man's interaction with God regarding receiving His wealth. This will begin the fourth key to unlock Heaven's wealth for you.

Always remember that, according to God's Word, giving and receiving link together. Think about this: Let's say you find a bank, which pays an annual return of 300% in interest. All you must do to be eligible for the 300% return is first open an account with a deposit and establish that the funds are yours (such as with a signature card and possibly your photo identification). Then, you would be on your way to earning 300%. Also, you could withdraw some of the funds from the account. However, you would need to prove your identity first. This is similar to depositing in and withdrawing from God's heavenly bank account.

Let's examine His Word and begin the correct actions of deposit and withdrawal. In this book, my emphasis is the word *mentality*. Get ready for an attitude check! The following points contain attitudes, viewpoints, actions, and conversations that influence the release of wealth from God to you.

Put God to the test to determine that indeed He will fulfill His Word. To be certain that God will fulfill His Word, prove Him. However, before He performs His promises, you must do your part! Let's revisit the book of Malachi:

> Bring ye all the tithes into the storehouse, that there may be meat in mine house, and *prove me now herewith*, saith the LORD of hosts, if I will not open you the windows of heaven, and pour you out a blessing, that there shall not be room enough to receive it.
>
> And I will rebuke the devourer for your sakes, and he shall not destroy the fruits of your ground; neither shall your vine cast her fruit before the time in the field, saith the LORD of hosts.
>
> And all nations shall call you blessed: for ye shall be a delightsome land, saith the LORD of hosts.
>
> Malachi 3:10-12

When you give, connect your heart to your giving. Place a demand upon the integrity of God's Word, believing that He will perform what He promised. This is not a one-time experience but a continual state of knowing in your heart that God does fulfill His Word. Then, you will not be afraid to trust Him. By experience, you will *know* that God is always faithful to you.

Give directly to God without negative words. On earth, the way we give to God is through Godly ministries usually. Sometimes, however, these organizations disappoint us in how they handle our donations. This challenge often causes many to abort their own prosperity unknowingly. *Never, never, never speak negatively or in frustration regarding your financial gifts.* Always tell God that you are giving your money to *Him,* and no one on earth owes you a return on it. Your multiplied yield comes from God alone. Yes, He does use people. However, you must not limit whom He can use. Remember, earlier we studied that while we physically pay our tithes to mortal men, the Lord actually receives them.

Now, once you have given, guard your tongue! God is listening:

"You have said harsh things against me," says the LORD. "Yet you ask, 'What have we said against you?'

"You have said, '*It is futile to serve God*. What did we gain by carrying out his requirements and going about like mourners before the LORD Almighty?

But now *we call the arrogant blessed. Certainly the evildoers prosper, and even those who challenge God escape.'*"

Then those who feared the LORD talked with each other, and the LORD listened and heard.

Malachi 3:13-16 (NIV)

In the King James Version, the last verse above reads:

Then they that feared the LORD spake often one to another: and the LORD hearkened, and heard it, and a book of remembrance was written before him for them that feared the LORD, and that thought upon his name.

Malachi 3:16

Be sure to stay blessed. Remember, Proverbs 18:21:

Death and life are in the power of the tongue: and they that love it shall eat the fruit thereof.

Proverbs 18:21

Always give liberally with an attitude of gratitude! Your attitude makes a tremendous difference when you give to the Lord. The Apostle Paul said:

> But this I say, He which soweth sparingly shall reap also sparingly; and he which soweth bountifully shall reap also bountifully.
>
> *Every man according as he purposeth in his heart,* so let him give; *not grudgingly,* or *of necessity:* for *God loveth a cheerful giver.*
>
> And God is able to make all grace abound toward you; that ye, always having all sufficiency in all things, may abound to every good work:
>
> (As it is written, He hath dispersed abroad; he hath given to the poor: his righteousness remaineth for ever.
>
> Now he that ministereth seed to the sower both minister bread for your food, and multiply your seed sown, and increase the fruits of your righteousness.)
>
> 2 Corinthians 9:6-10

The following verses clearly state that God freely gives riches for our enjoyment, but with these blessings He commands us to give generously:

> Command those who are rich in this present world not to be arrogant nor to put their hope in wealth, which is so uncertain, but to put their hope in God, who richly provides us with everything for our enjoyment.
>
> Command them to do good, to be rich in good deeds, and to be generous and willing to share.
>
> In this way they will lay up treasure for themselves as a firm foundation for the coming age, so that they may

take hold of the life that is truly life.

1 Timothy 6:17-19 (NIV)

Expect to receive. This is where many falter and are uncertain, wondering *How do I receive from God?*

In the Amplified Bible, I believe that Philippians 4:13-19 says it best:

> I have strength for all things in Christ Who empowers me—I am ready for anything and equal to anything through Him Who infuses inner strength into me, [that is, I am self-sufficient in Christ's sufficiency).
>
> But it was right and commendable and noble of you to contribute for my needs and to share my difficulties with me.
>
> And you Philippians yourselves well know that in the early days of the Gospel ministry, when I left Macedonia, no such church (assembly) *entered into partnership with me and opened up [a debit and credit] account in giving and receiving except you only.*
>
> For even in Thessalonica you sent [me contributions] for my needs, not only once but a second time.
>
> Not that I seek or am eager for [your] gift, but I do seek and am eager for the fruit which increases to your credit—the harvest of blessing that is accumulating to your account.
>
> But I have [your full payment] and more; I have everything I need and am amply supplied, now that I have received from Epaphroditus the gifts you sent me. [They are the] fragrant odor of an offering and sacrifice which God welcomes and in which He delights.
>
> And my God will liberally supply (fill to the full)

your every need according to His riches in glory in Christ Jesus.

Philippians 4:13-19 (AMP)

Now, if you know that God has an account in Heaven, through which you can deposit and withdraw wealth, then use it! This is what Jesus meant when He instructed us to lay up for ourselves treasures in Heaven. This account is multiplying and reserved for only you!

Never allow doubt to affect your confidence. Speak boldly that only the Lord is your Source and Supply! God encouraged Abraham after he had tithed and declared that God would receive all the glory for making him rich:

After these things the word of the LORD came unto Abram in a vision, saying, Fear not, Abram: I am thy shield, and *thy exceeding great reward.*

Genesis 15:1

The act of receiving is to be your everyday routine. After all, did not Jesus teach us to pray for God to "give us this day our daily bread"? In what we know today as The Lord's Prayer, Jesus said:

After this manner therefore pray ye: Our Father which art in heaven, Hallowed be thy name.

Thy kingdom come. Thy will be done in earth, as it is in heaven.

Give us this day our daily bread.

And forgive us our debts, as we forgive our debtors.

And lead us not into temptation, but deliver us from evil: For thine is the kingdom, and the power, and the glory, for ever. Amen.

Matthew 6:9-13

Then in the same chapter of Matthew, remember Jesus declared:

But seek ye first the kingdom of God, and his righteousness; and all these things shall be added unto you.

Matthew 6:33

Every day is the time to receive!

A Mountain-Moving Testimony

Now, I have a special blessing for you. Let me close this last chapter with a moving story of a Christian businessman. After this young man learned the true purpose of wealth and began to practice God's principles, his life was never the same. It can happen for you, too!

Many probably thought nothing much would become of Bobby, the rebellious "black sheep" of the LeTourneau family. One book described his beginnings as: "A *Grade School* drop-out. A *Run Away* from home at fourteen."[5] When he left home, LeTourneau accepted a job in a foundry shoveling sand and became an iron molder. However, the boy's Christian parents, who had trained him in the ways of the Lord, did not give up. Instead, they released their son to God and continued to pray for his salvation.

Two years later, at 16 years of age, the young LeTourneau accepted Jesus Christ as his personal Lord and Savior. That one decision forever changed his life *and the world.* You see, this is

141

the story of Robert Gilmour LeTourneau (1888-1969), internationally known inventor, entrepreneur, educator, and philanthropist. "He has been credited with the creation of the modern mechanized earthmoving industry."[6] This unique man held more than 430 patents and is rated as one of the top 20 inventors in history.[7] He created nearly 300 inventions including the individual electric motor, the electric wheel, bridge spans, the bulldozer, a forerunner to the modern earthmovers, the offshore drilling platform, and much more. "He was the first major manufacturer to make welding a universally accepted process."[8] (Remember, I was once a welder in a factory!)

"Nearly every type of modern heavy earthmoving equipment owes its design to R.G. LeTourneau."[9] His machines revolutionized the industries of heavy construction, mining, logging, land clearing, and offshore oil drilling. LeTourneau eventually operated manufacturing plants in California, Illinois, Georgia, Mississippi, and Texas.

During World War II, the LeTourneau Company built 70% of the earthmoving equipment, which the Allies used.[10] At the height of the war, from 1942 to 1945, R.G. created "78 inventions, many of which were instrumental in helping to win the war."[11] In 1953, the Westinghouse Air Brake Company bought R.G. LeTourneau's designs and business for more than $30 million.[12]

Additionally, R.G. together with his beloved wife, Evelyn, opened the LeTourneau Technical Institute in 1946, which has since grown to become a widely acclaimed Christian institution called LeTourneau University. *U.S. News and World Report* has ranked it as one of America's best colleges.[13]

The school began when Mom and Pop LeTourneau, as many called them, had a burden to help their factory workers and the returning GIs from World War II. Since these young people needed further education and spiritual ministry, the

LeTourneaus started educational and spiritual training programs in their factories. This proved to be the forerunner of LeTourneau University, which has produced more than 10,000 alumni, who have reached out to serve God throughout the U.S.A. and 55 nations. This accredited Christian university offers degree programs today in engineering, technology, liberal arts, business, aviation, education and the sciences, plus master's programs in business administration and business management.[14] Think about it: God produced all this from a grade-school drop-out!

On the occasion of the university's fiftieth anniversary in 1996, Former President George Bush said of R.G. LeTourneau, "He was always willing to push the envelope. He was willing to follow his vision. Just as your namesake was committed to excellence, just as he was an innovative leader, so too has LeTourneau University become an institution known for its dedication to principles and its vision.... Keep up the terrific work!"

Former President Bush had become well acquainted with R.G. decades earlier after buying LeTourneau's first newly invented offshore drilling platforms. The former President of the United States "credits R.G.'s offshore rig with enabling him to gain the wealth and freedom to become involved in politics"![15] Do you realize the impact one person can have when simply following God's dream in his heart?

Deciding to keep their priorities in order regarding money, Evelyn and R.G. "established the LeTourneau Foundation and placed ninety percent of the corporation stock in the Foundation, so that stock dividends went to the Foundation instead of to them personally. The earnings from the Foundation stock would then be used in Christian endeavors around the world.

"Resources from the Foundation enabled Evelyn to purchase

five acres on Winona Lake, Indiana, where she established Camp Bethany in 1937. She enlisted students and graduates of Wheaton College to serve as counselors and speakers, one of whom was a young preacher named Billy Graham."[16] Years later, his son, Franklin, attended LeTourneau University and returned recently as the featured speaker at the class of 2000 Commencement exercise.

In the book *LeTourneau University's First Fifty Years*, board member Billy Graham wrote in the foreword, "In my judgment, LeTourneau is one of the finest schools combining academics, Christian witness and technical expertise that I know about. LeTourneau University's great advantage lies in its philosophy of linking the academic and the spiritual with a practical approach. Led by the example of its founders, it produces a 'faith at work' that permeates every course and impacts every student."

In the early days, R.G. and Evelyn LeTourneau struggled with the desire to serve God full-time and build a business. At that point, God used their pastor to encourage them, who told them that God needs both businessmen and preachers. "This idea revolutionized their lives. R.G. became a mover of men and spent the next 30 years traveling the world helping build the Kingdom of God at his own expense." Because of his earthmoving equipment, R.G. was also known as a mover of mountains.[17]

It all began at age 30, when he dedicated himself to be a "businessman for God." However, his love for building machines, "never deterred him from what he felt was his reason for existence: to glorify God and spread the Gospel message."[18] "One of five founders of the Christian Business Men International,"[19] R.G. "is widely recognized...as the moving force behind bringing Christianity and the business world into a working relationship on many fronts."[20]

How did all this come about? R.G. LeTourneau attributed his rise from drop-out to millionaire entirely to God. He claimed that he was foremost a Christian.

> I've always said when people ask me about the inventions I've come up with, that anything I've been able to do I credit to God Who gave me my mind.... I Corinthians 2:9 says, "Eye hath not seen, nor ear heard, neither have entered into the heart of man, the things which God hath prepared for them that love Him." Man can't comprehend such wonders with his natural mind—can't imagine it—but the next verse says, "But God hath revealed them unto us by His Spirit." So if you want to enter into the wonders of God, don't try to do it with man's natural mind, but accept God's Son as your Savior and let the Holy Spirit show you the wonders of a life in God, both for now and for eternity."[21]

Thousands of times around the world, he told audiences:

> My life verse has been Matthew 6:33, "Seek ye first the kingdom of God and His righteousness and all these things shall be added unto you."[22]

Throughout R.G.'s life wherever he spoke, he began his messages with statements such as: "Friends, I'm just a sinner that's been saved by the grace of God—just a mechanic that the Lord has blessed....He saved me by His grace and made me His child."[23] "But my machines and my accomplishments," he once said, "seem mighty small when I look up into the Heavens at night—and they tell me those stars are bigger than this world...—

and then I realize how small I am and wonder that God would send His Son to save me and help me."[24]

He usually spoke not only of his inventions and other matters of the business, but also about how these physical things paralleled God's spiritual principles. For example, in 1948, he said:

...May I call to attention, the contrast between the Scripture story of creation and my story of earthmoving invention?

I have said, "In the beginning I developed." So must every inventor, engineer and designer say, "I developed" or "I made." Even if it is an original invention in a virgin field it must be made from something that already exists....

"In the beginning God created." See the difference in those first five words of the Bible. Man must start with something, but God began with nothing, absolute nothing, and "created the heaven and the earth." As we have it in the Gospel of John, "All things were made by Him; and without Him was not any thing made that was made." So whether it be producing a world or a universe from nothing, or making man from the dust of the ground and breathing into his nostrils the breath of life, or making the clod of the earth from which man was shaped, God is the Creator or Maker.

Had He begun with matter which another had provided, He would not be God. Having begun with nothing, nothing is for Him impossible. He could furnish the heavens with universes which men could discover only with the telescope and thereby picture the construction of the atom which they cannot see with a microscope.

Our best action then is to bow the knee as Job and say, "I know that Thou canst do everything."[25]

Because of his love for God, R.G. LeTourneau founded missionary efforts in Liberia, West Africa and in Peru, South America, where he personally invested millions of dollars. Because of this, countless thousands heard the Gospel, and received education and medical aid.[26]

In 1956, R.G. LeTourneau explained his views on wealth:

It doesn't make any difference how much money you have; you can only sleep in one bed at a time, and you can only wear one suit of clothes at a time, and I know you can't eat any more than I, so let's quit our worrying and remember we can't take it with us; but we can give it to the Lord's work and the Word of God says that we will have treasures in Heaven, so I say we can send it on ahead and have it waiting for us when we get there.[27]

Near the end of his life, R.G. LeTourneau said regarding tithing:

I've never been much of a preacher on tithing.... My motto has been—Not how much of my money do I give to God but how much of God's money do I keep for myself.

I hope you are now beginning to understand what I meant when I began by saying that I'm not much of a preacher of tithing. If under the law the people of God gave one-tenth to the Lord, shame on us living under grace, if we don't do better. The tithe may be a place to begin if you are not now giving to the Lord, but it's no place to stop. You see what I mean. If you get a vision of what our salvation cost, see Christ on the cross, the cruel nails in His hands and feet, the mocking crowd and the weight of our sin paying the penalty for you and for me, it will put your service and giving on a different plane. He gave Himself willingly to give us salvation from our sin. If this grips us, we can't help but love Him....

True love based on an understanding of God's grace, deep gratitude for the gift of salvation through our Lord will settle the problem of "what I should give to God" because my thinking will be turned around to consider that all I am and have belong to Him, and I am a steward for Him while serving Him in this life.[28]

In paying tribute to R.G. on his seventieth birthday, his son, Richard, recounted the Christian principles, which he saw his father follow to success:

1. First of all he has a deep desire to do the will of the Lord whatever it may be and is willing to accept the will of the Lord without question....

2. Secondly, he has a tremendous faith that the Lord will overcome all problems and difficulties in His own time and in His own manner....

3. His sole purpose in life is to serve the Lord in whatever way the Lord would have him do so....

4. In operation of the business, he believes that most men are, or at least should be, interested in the work they are doing and not just an 8 to 5 or 7 to 3:30 clock

puncher....

5. In dealing with personnel, he can forgive and forget a thousand-dollar mistake if the individual admits it was a mistake and makes no attempt to cover it up....

6. Lastly, to everyone who is close to him, he is one who "practices what he preaches"....[29]

In a report on R.G. LeTourneau's memorial service, the *Longview Daily News and Journal* included:

Basing his remarks on the life of Mr. LeTourneau on Acts 13:36, Dr. Harvey said, "Robert Gilmour LeTourneau structured his life on the principles that a man must know God, a man must know the will of God, and a man must carry out the will of God. Mr. LeTourneau believed with all his heart that God had a message for him and the most fitting epitaph for this great man is that he served his generation by the will of God.

"His driving force was to get all men to know God as he did, for God was real to him...and he talked to God with the ease of sure knowledge, at any time and any place."[30]

After the memorial service, one of R.G. LeTourneau's employees wrote:

How do we account for a ministry of such scope by one couple? Maybe this explains it: Mr. R.G., speaking to a men's meeting, said, "You will never know what you can accomplish, what your potential is, until you say A GREAT BIG 'YES' TO GOD."

...In answer to the question of how we can know God's will for our lives, Mr. R.G. often answers, "You don't need to know that. If you have a guide Whom you trust, you do not need to know the destination to follow Him. Simply take the NEXT STEP with Him; put your trust in Him in all the details of life."[31]

In his autobiography, R.G. LeTourneau wrote:

For 25 years or more, I've been traveling this land of ours and a few foreign countries trying to teach and preach by word of mouth and example, that a Christian businessman owes as much to God as a preacher does. The rest of the time I build machinery, almost any kind of machinery as long as it is big, and powerful, and can move around to do things no other machine could do before. Some people think I'm all mixed up—that you can't serve the Lord and business, too, but that's just the point. God needs businessmen as partners as well as preachers. When He created the world and everything in it, He didn't mean for us to stop there and say, "God, You've done it all. There's nothing left for us to build." He wanted us to take off from there and really build for His greater glory."[32]

Upon R.G. LeTourneau's death in 1969, the *New York Times* published a story about the "internationally known manufacturer of earthmoving equipment," which included the following:

Robert Gilmour LeTourneau liked to do two things: "One is to design machines, turn on the power and see them work; the other is to help turn on the power of the Gospel and see it work in people's lives."

He did both in a big way.

Mr. LeTourneau was the developer and manufacturer of the world's largest earthmoving machinery. He was also a crusading evangelist who regularly traveled more than 200,000 miles a year preaching. His motto was "God is my partner.... God is chairman of my board of directors."

Mr. LeTourneau believed that "a factory can be dedicated to God as well as a church and that it may be used as a means of saving many souls."[33]

Once R.G. LeTourneau shared a story about visiting a diamond mine in Belgium Congo, after the owner had written to him asking if he had a machine that would improve the company's efficiency. As R.G. toured the operation, God gave revelation knowledge to him. He saw the diamond-mining process with spiritual eyes, and said:

>...The Bible likens our work down here for the Lord, to gold, silver and precious stones. It will be tried by fire and the wood, hay and stubble will be burned up; so I want my work to be like a jewel, a diamond if you please, for the Lord....
>
> I believe God is handpicking out of this wicked world a people that will sparkle for him in the ages to come, some out of every kindred, tongue, people and nation. And they will sing a new song in heaven, Revelation 5:9."[34]

Are you a diamond for God? Will you allow Him to

sparkle through you?

Remember, His purpose for your life includes prosperity, not only for you but also for His Kingdom's work.

Look for your dream seeds—those giftings or talents that God has planted in you as seeds of His Prophetic Vision. Nurture them. Begin to pursue His vision. Become pregnant with God's dream, as you meditate on it and His Word. Declare the Word and God's provision over your life. When you do, you will find God's field for you, and the blessings of wealth will follow. Thus, your Heavenly Father will provide the way for you to achieve His purpose and find true fulfillment. Then, you can bless the work of the Lord.

Now, you know the principles for obtaining a *Millionaire Mentality*. What will you do with this information? Will you allow it to change your life so you can provide for your family and become a cash pump for the Kingdom of God? It's your choice. The entire world is awaiting your decision. Go for it!

Notes

Chapter 4

[1] Gary DeMar, *God and Government: A Biblical and Historical Study*, vol. 1 (Georgia: American Vision Press), p. 126.

[2] *Compton's Interactive Encyclopedia Deluxe* © 1998 (The Learning Company, Inc.).

[3] Ibid.

[4] *World Book Millennium 2000* (World Book, Inc.).

Chapter 8

[5] Nels E. Stjernstrom, *The Joy of Accomplishment* (Longview: LeTourneau University), p. 20.

[6] LeTourneau University web site: http://www.letu.edu.

[7] *LeTourneau University: The First 50 Years*, dir. Dean Waskowiak and Ron Matchett, Encore Multimedia, 1996.

[8] Ibid.

[9] Ibid.

[10] Stjernstrom, backcover (from a historical marker in Longview, Texas, which commemorates the accomplishments of R.G. LeTourneau). LeTourneau University web site.

[11] LeTourneau University web site.

[12] Louise LeTourneau Dick, *R.G. Talks About...: The Industrial Genius, Practical Philisophy, and Christian Commitment of Robert G. LeTourneau (1888-1969)*, (Longview: LeTourneau Press), p. 250.

[13] Waskowiak and Matchett.

[14] LeTourneau University web site.

[15] Waskowiak and Matchett.

[16] Kenneth Durham, *LeTourneau University's First Fity Years*, chapter 1 online at LeTourneau University web site.

[17] Waskowiak and Matchett.

[18] LeTourneau University web site.

[19] Dick, p. 252.

[20] Ibid., p. 8.

[21] Ibid., p. 244.

[22] Ibid., p. 246.

[23] LeTourneau University web site (excerpt from R.G. LeTourneau's audio message on August 16, 1967 in Myrtle, Mississippi).

[24] Dick, p. 219.

[25] Ibid., p. 48.

[26] LeTourneau University web site.

[27] Dick, p. 148.

[28] Ibid., pp. 246-247.

[29] Ibid., pp. 9-12.

[30] Ibid., pp. 252-253.

[31] Ibid., 239.

[32] R.G. LeTourneau, *R.G. LeTourneau: Mover of Men and Mountains* (Chicago: Moody Press), p. 1.

[33] Dick, pp. 248-250.

[34] Ibid., pp. 230-232.

Grow by Becoming God's Child

How to Receive God's Free Gift

Have you ever received God's free gift of Eternal Life? Do you know for certain that if you were to die today you would go to Heaven? Everlasting life is a gift from God. When Jesus Christ died on the cross and rose bodily from the grave, He paid for our sins. The Bible says:

> For God so loved the world, that he gave his only begotten Son, that whosoever believeth in him should not perish, but have everlasting life.
>
> John 3:16

Since Jesus paid for this gift, we don't have to. We only need to receive it.

> But as many as received him, to them gave he power to become the sons of God, even to them that believe on his name.
>
> John 1:12

> For by grace are ye saved through faith; and that not of yourselves: it is the gift of God:
> Not of works, lest any man should boast.
>
> Ephesians 2:8-9

The way to receive God's gift simply is to believe God's Word and receive it by the profession of your mouth.

> That if you confess with your mouth, "Jesus is Lord," and believe in your heart that God raised him from the dead, you will be saved.
> For it is with your heart that you believe and are justified, and it is with your mouth that you confess and are saved.
>
> Romans 10:9-10 (NIV)

Now, pray this prayer aloud:

> **Father, thank You for loving me. Thank You for giving Your Son, Jesus, to die and to raise from the dead for me.**
> **Jesus Christ, Son of God, come into my heart, forgive me of my sins, and be my Lord and Savior. Jesus, I declare that You are Lord, and that You are Lord of my life. In Jesus' Name. Amen.**

You are now born again!

All believers are entitled to over 7,000 promises that God has written in His Word. That now includes you! To learn about these promises, attend church regularly. If you are in the area of New Castle, Delaware, please join us for services at Victory Christian Fellowship. Visit our web site at www.gwwm.com for directions and more information. I encourage you to attend a local church that teaches the uncompromised Word of God—the Bible. Daily spend time in prayer, fellowship with the Lord, and reading the Bible. This will help you to understand the "new creature" that you have become now in Christ.

> ...If any man be in Christ, he is a *new creature:* old things are passed away; behold, all things are become new.
>
> 2 Corinthians 5:17

For more information about your new life in Christ, please order *The Victorious Walk* book. *Purchase this book wherever fine Christian products are sold in your area. Or, see the product list and order form at the back of this book.*

Grow by Receiving God's Spirit

Have You Received the Holy Spirit Since You Believed?

In Acts 19:2 (NKJV), the apostle Paul asked the Ephesians this very important question:

> "Did you receive the Holy Spirit when you believed?"

The question startled them, and they answered:

> "We have not so much as heard whether there is a Holy Spirit."

Later, when they prayed together:

> ...The Holy Spirit came on them, and they spoke in tongues and prophesied.
>
> Acts 19:6 (NIV)

What Is the Baptism in the Holy Spirit?

The Baptism in the Holy Spirit is an anointing of power, an enabling or ability from God in the believer's life, which equips him or her to witness fully of the life of Jesus Christ.

The Holy Spirit was given on the Day of Pentecost and has

never left. This is a distinct experience from conversion to Christ. The Baptism in the Holy Spirit was a separate experience in Jesus' life when He was water baptized, in the apostles' lives on the Day of Pentecost, and in the believer's life today.

Who Is It for, and What Is It?

The Baptism in the Holy Spirit is for believers, because the world cannot receive Him. This experience is to equip and empower believers to worship God supernaturally. The first move of the Holy Spirit when He came upon the early Christians was to speak the praises of God through them (Acts 2:11).

This Baptism is God's outpouring of His Spirit into a person's life to equip him or her to be a witness of Jesus. Christ said:

> But ye shall receive power, after that the Holy Ghost is come upon you: and ye shall be witnesses unto me both in Jerusalem, and in all Judaea, and in Samaria, and unto the uttermost part of the earth.
>
> Acts 1:8

Why Be Baptized in the Holy Spirit?

It is God's will for every believer to be baptized in the Holy Spirit. It is His desire that you overflow with His Spirit continually. Jesus COMMANDED the disciples not to leave Jerusalem until they had been endued with power.

> And, behold, I send the promise of my Father upon you: but tarry ye in the city of Jerusalem, until ye be endued with power from on high.
>
> Luke 24:49

In Ephesians 5:17-18, the Word of God says that believers are to understand (comprehend, grasp, perceive) what the will of the Lord is. Also, they are to be filled with the Holy Spirit.

> Wherefore be ye not unwise, but understanding what the will of the Lord is.
> And be not drunk with wine, wherein is excess; but be filled with the Spirit.
>
> Ephesians 5:17-18

Jesus also said those who believe on Him SHOULD receive the Holy Spirit:

> (But this spake he of the Spirit, which they that believe on him should receive: for the Holy Ghost was not yet given; because that Jesus was not yet glorified.)
>
> John 7:39

How Do I Receive the Baptism in the Holy Spirit?

Ask and you will receive. Knowing that it is God's will for us to be filled with the Holy Spirit gives us confidence in asking Him to baptize us in the Holy Spirit.

> And this is the confidence that we have in him, that, if we ask any thing according to his will, he heareth us:
> ...If we know that he hear us, whatsoever we ask, we know that we have the petitions that we desired of him.
>
> 1 John 5:14-15

> ...Ask, and it shall be given you...

...how much more shall your heavenly Father give the Holy Spirit to them that ask him?

Luke 11:9, 13

What Happens when I Receive this Baptism?

New Language

One of the first experiences that we have when we are filled with the Holy Spirit is that God gives to us a supernatural language. Our hearts are turned more completely to God, to whom we were reconciled already in Jesus Christ when we were born again. Jesus said:

And these signs shall follow them that believe...they shall speak with new tongues.

Mark 16:17

The Gentiles in the house of Cornelius spoke with tongues when the Holy Spirit came on them (Acts 10:44-48). Likewise, as we studied earlier, the people of Ephesus spoke in tongues when the Holy Spirit came upon them:

And when Paul had laid hands on them, the Holy Spirit came upon them, and they spoke with tongues and prophesied.

Acts 19:6 (NKJV)

What Does Speaking in Tongues Do?

Praises the Lord in a God-Appointed Way

...When thou shalt bless with the spirit...

...thou verily givest thanks well....

1 Corinthians 14:16-17

Edifies Spiritually

He that speaketh in an unknown tongue edifieth himself.

1 Corinthians 14:4a

Reminds of the Holy Spirit's Indwelling Presence

"And I will pray the Father, and He will give you another Helper, that He may abide with you forever,

"even the Spirit of truth, whom the world cannot receive, because it neither sees Him nor knows Him; but you know Him, for He dwells with you and will be in you."

John 14:16-17 (NKJV)

Prays in Line with God's Perfect Will

Likewise the Spirit also helpeth our infirmities: for we know not what we should pray for as we ought: but the Spirit itself maketh intercession for us with groanings which cannot be uttered.

And he that searcheth the hearts knoweth what is the mind of the Spirit, because he maketh intercession for the saints according to the will of God.

Romans 8:26-27

Stimulates Faith

But ye, beloved, building up yourselves on your

most holy faith, praying in the Holy Ghost.

Jude 1:20

Refreshes Spiritually

For with stammering lips and another tongue will he speak to this people.

To whom he said, This is the rest wherewith ye may cause the weary to rest; and this is the refreshing: yet they would not hear.

Isaiah 28:11-12

Opens Your Prayer Line to God

For he that speaketh in an unknown tongue speaketh not unto men, but unto God: for no man understandeth him; howbeit in the spirit he speaketh mysteries.

For if I pray in an unknown tongue, my spirit prayeth, but my understanding is unfruitful.

1 Corinthians 14:2, 14

Please pray this prayer aloud now:

Father, thank You that at the moment I ask to be filled with the Holy Spirit, I will be filled. The evidence is that I will speak with other tongues by my will, though I will not understand with my mind. Now, Father, fill me with the Holy Spirit, in the Name of Jesus. Thank You for filling me. I have received, now. By a decision of my will, I speak to You in other tongues. In Jesus' Name. Amen.

We can build ourselves up and speak to God wherever we

are—in the car, riding the bus or airplane, at home, or on the job. It will not disturb anyone. Speaking in tongues is a means of keeping free from the contamination of the world.

Supernatural Gifts of Power

The gifts of the Holy Spirit can begin now to operate in and through your life. According to 1 Corinthians 12:7-11, the nine gifts of the Spirit are:

- Word of Wisdom
- Word of Knowledge
- Discerning of Spirits
- Prophecy
- Diversity of Tongues
- Interpretation of Tongues
- Special Faith
- Healings
- Working of Miracles

For more information about how to live as a victorious Christian, please order *The Victorious Walk* book. *Purchase this book wherever fine Christian products are sold in your area. Or, see the product list and order form at the back of this book.*

Grow by Knowing God's Word

Become a Student of God's Word with The School of Biblical Studies

Destroy Your #1 Enemy

Your #1 Enemy is on the prowl!

Your #1 Enemy knows more than you know!

Your #1 Enemy keeps you from complete fulfillment!

Your #1 Enemy has destroyed your past!

Your #1 Enemy breaks up families!

Your #1 Enemy is always with you!

Your #1 Enemy is.........shhhhhhhh! Don't tell anybody

Your #1 Enemy is ignorance!

What you **DON'T KNOW** will hurt you!

Don't let it destroy your future like it has your past!

Remember that God's Word declares:

My people are destroyed for lack of knowledge: because thou hast rejected knowledge, I will also reject thee....

Hosea 4:6

Turn the page to find an exciting offer for a free video CD, for your computer or DVD player, which will change your life! (Of course, you may instead order an audio cassette or a video cassette in VHS-NTSC.)

Ignorance!!!!!!!!! You are destroyed NOW!!!!!!!!!

165

The School of Biblical Studies brings to life powerful truths that will unlock personal fulfillment in your God-given vision, family, finances, health, mental well-being, prayer, and much more.

By contacting Gary Whetstone Worldwide Ministries today, you will begin a journey into practical and simple answers. You won't believe how much you have missed all of these years. These impactive teachings bring to light the power of God's revelation knowledge and set you above all that is average and ordinary.

Study Options

Attend The School of Biblical Studies extension school in your own home through any of the following:

1. Audio cassettes
2. Video cassettes (VHS-NTSC only)
3. Audio CDs for CD players, computer CD-ROM drives, and most DVD players
4. CD-ROM videos for use on most personal computer CD-ROM drives
5. Video CDs (VCDs) for viewing on video CD and recent DVD players

Or attend a Branch Bible School in a classroom setting offered in hundreds of locations throughout the United States and abroad. All students receive the same courses and curriculum as those at the main campus location in New Castle, Delaware.

Certificate and Diploma

A certificate and diploma will be awarded upon graduation from the junior and senior years of Biblical Studies. These units of study also may be transferred to a degree program.

Order today your free sample class on *Your Liberty in Christ!*

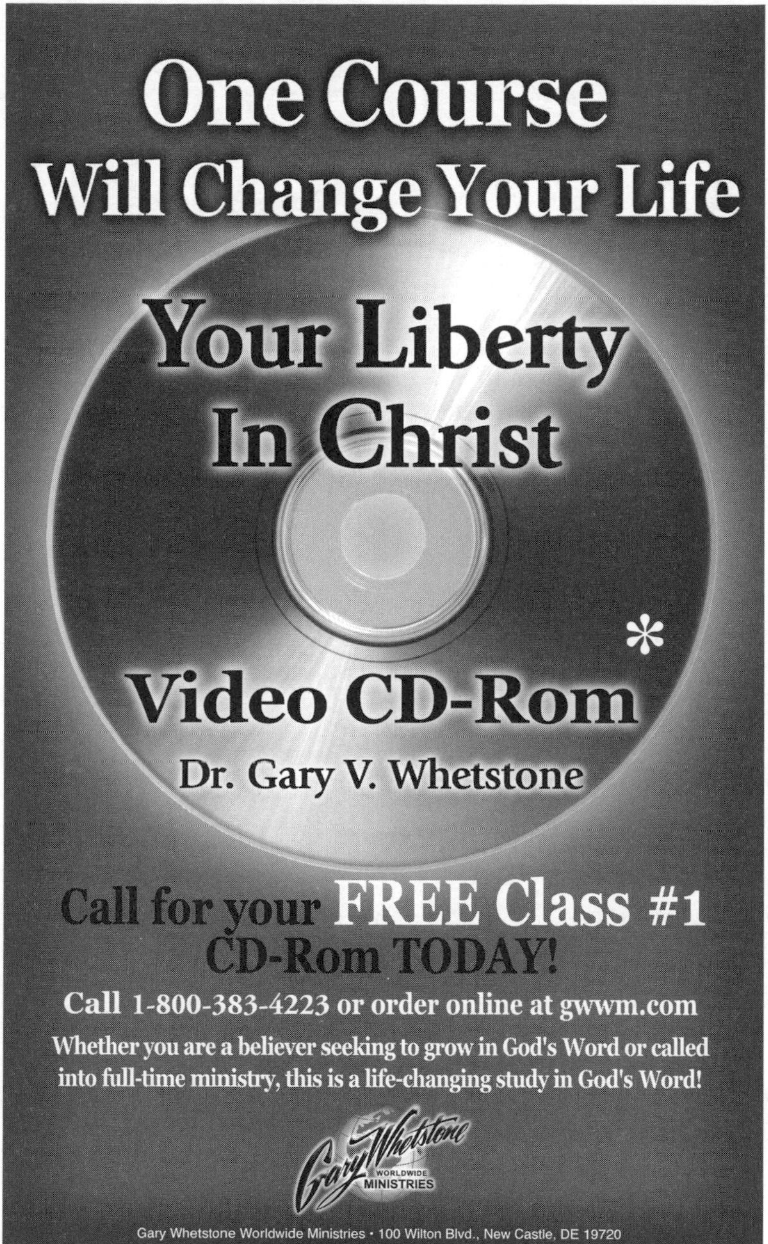

*Also available in audio cassette,
audio CD, and video CD

Dr. Gary V. Whetstone

What will you do with God's call on your life?

Find God's Answer Through:

School of Victorious Living

Face life's challenges with proven biblical answers!
Audio/video teachings with study guides available for study in your own home. May be purchased online at gwwm.com/gwwm-frames.htm.

School of Biblical Studies

Establish a closer relationship with God!
Gain a deeper understanding of His Word.
In-depth Bible school curriculum for serious students of God's Word. Available in classroom settings at hundreds of churches or for study in your home on audio cassette, videotape, CD, CD-ROM, and VCD.

School of Ministerial Training

Called into full-time ministry?
Pastor/Teacher • Evangelist/Missionary
Church Helps • Music Ministry
Receive hands-on training along with classroom instruction.

Contact us for more information and to receive a free brochure. See our web site for course descriptions and free downloads of sample lessons.

Gary Whetstone Worldwide Ministries
P.O. Box 10050, Wilmington, DE 19850 U.S.A.
PHONE: 1 (302) 324-5400 • FAX: 1 (302) 324-5448
WEB SITE: www.gwwm.com
E-MAIL: info@gwwm.com

School of Victorious Living

The following is a partial listing of Gary Whetstone's teaching series on video and audio tapes available for your study and spiritual growth. **For a detailed catalog of materials from the School of Victorious Living, please visit our web site or contact us at:**

Gary Whetstone Worldwide Ministries
P.O. Box 10050
Wilmington, DE 19850-0050 U.S.A.
Phone: 1 (302) 324-5400   Fax: 1 (302) 324-5448
Web Site: www.gwwm.com   E-mail: info@gwwm.com

Empowerment Series

These power-packed courses equip you for your successful Christian walk as you fulfill God's will and purpose for your life.

Character—The Only Concrete Worth Building On	Audio(VE003A) $35; Video (VE003V) $50
Commissioned Under Command	Audio (VE004A) $35; Video (VE004V) $50
Commitment to Completion	Audio (VE005A) $35; Video (VE005V) $50
Effective Praise	Audio (VE007A) $35
How to Heal the Sick	Audio (VE009A) $20; Video (VE009V) $30
It's Time to Seek the Lord	Audio (VE012A) $35
Know the Real You	Audio (VE013A) $35
Mobilizing Believers	Audio (VE014A) $50; Video (VE014V) $85
Move with the Holy Spirit in Gifts and Power	Audio (VE015A) $50; Video (VE015V) $75
Preparing for the End Times	Audio (VE016A) $40
The Call of God	Audio (VE002A) $35
The Power of God's Prophetic Purpose	English audio, study guide (VE029A) $50; Spanish audio, no study guide (VE030A) $25
The Prevailing Power of Prayer	Audio (VE010A) $50
The Unshakable Foundation	Audio (VE018A) $60
What Is this Revival, Anyway?	Audio (VE019A) $35
What Is Your Gospel?	Audio (VE017A) $35
Which Path Do I Take?	Audio (VE020A) $35

Freedom Series

The revelation you will receive about using God's weapons for victorious living will set you free from every offense, attack, and distress the enemy tries to wage against you.

Assignment Against the Church: Spirit of Offense	Audio (VR001A) $50
Blood-Bought Promises	Audio (VR002A) $35; Video (VR002V) $50
Discovering God's Highway to Your Destiny	Audio (VE006A) $35

Extracting the Gold	
from Life's Crises	Audio (VR003A) $35; Video (VR003V) $50
Freedom from	
Insecurity and Inferiority	Audio (VR004A) $50; Video (VR004V) $75
How to Harness Your Mind	Audio (VR011A) $35
How to Identify	
and Remove Curses	Audio (VR005A) $50; Video (VR005V) $75
Love's Transforming Power	Audio (VR007A) $35; Video (VR007V) $50
Make Fear Bow	Audio (VR008A) $35
The Journey from Frustration	
to Fulfillment	Audio (VR006A) $50
The Power of the Lord's Blessing	Audio (VR009A) $35
Victory in Spiritual Warfare	Audio (VR010A) $60; Video (VR010V) $99

Family and Relationships Series

These series enable you to overcome conflicts, establish positive relationships, and bring God's visitation to your family.

God's Covenant	
with Your Family	Audio (VA007A) $35
How to Build	
the Communication Bridge	Audio (VA006A) $50
How to Fight for Your Family	Audio (VA001A) $60
Man Power: Challenge to	
the Man	Audio (VA002A) $50
Relationships: Your Ruin	
or Rejoicing	Audio (VA004A) $50
What God Has Joined Together	Audio (VA005A) $50; Video (VA005V) $75

Finance Series

Through these courses, learn how to reap your harvest and be set free forever from financial lack.

Champion, Success Is	
within Your Reach	**Audio (VI001A) $35; Video (VI001V) $50**
Freedom from Need-Domination	
through Purpose-Motivation	**Audio (VI002A) $35; Video (VI002V) $50**
Millionaire Mentality	**Audio (VI004A) $35; Video (VI004V) $50**
Purchasing & Negotiation	**Audio (VI008A) $50**
Reaping: Harvest Your Increase	**Audio (VI005A) $35**
Success in Business	**Audio (VI006A) $40; Video (VI006V) $65**
True Success—How to Find the	
Field God Planted for You	**Audio (VI007A) $35; Video (VI007V) $50**

Dig Deeper in Christ with these Life-Changing Books by Gary Whetstone

The following books are available wherever Christian products are sold in your area. Or order using the product catalog and form on our web site at *www.gwwm.com* or at the back of this book. Currently, these paperback books are available in various foreign languages or will be soon. Contact us for more information.

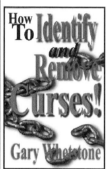

How to Identify and Remove Curses!

What you don't know *can* hurt you. Today, many Christians suffer unnecessary defeat, because they are unaware of their enemy's subtle tactics. This book provides practical, biblical steps to recognize and break unseen curses that could be holding you captive and destroying your life. Get ready for the Holy Spirit to set you free!

English	ISBN 0-9664462-1-6	VR005B	$9.00
Spanish	ISBN 0-9664462-5-9	VR005P	$9.00
French	ISBN 1-928774-04-0	VR006B	$9.00

Conquering Your Unseen Enemies

English	ISBN 0-9664462-2-4	VR013B	$12.99
Spanish	ISBN 0-9664462-6-7	VR014B	$12.99
French*	ISBN 1-928774-05-9	VR015B	$12.99

The Victorious Walk

English	ISBN 0-9664462-0-8	VE021B	$5.00
Spanish	ISBN 0-9664462-9-1	VE022B	$5.00
French	ISBN 1-928774-03-2	VE023B	$5.00

Life's Answers*

English	ISBN 0-9664462-7-5	VE027B
Spanish	ISBN 0-9664462-8-3	VE028B

Make Fear Bow*

English	ISBN 0-9664462-3-2	VR008B
Spanish	ISBN 1-928774-00-8	VR008S

Millionaire Mentality

English	ISBN 1-928774-01-6	VI004B	$14.99
Spanish*	ISBN 1-928774-02-4	VI004P	$14.99
French*	ISBN 1-928774-07-5	VI004F	$14.99

It Only Takes One*

English	VE031B
Spanish	VE031S

*Call for price and/or availability

Gary Whetstone Worldwide Ministries
P.O. Box 10050 • Wilmington, DE 19850 U.S.A.
P HONE:1 (302) 324-5400 • **E-MAIL:** info@gwwm.com
FAX: 1 (302) 324-5448 • **WEB SITE:** www.gwwm.com

Radio and TV Broadcasts

Gary Whetstone Worldwide Ministries
also reaches out daily across
parts of the United States,
Canada, and Europe
on radio, television,
and the Internet

For the TV or Radio
broadcast schedule
in your region,
call 1 (302) 324-5400
or E-mail info@gwwm.com

- Live on the Internet at www.gwwm.com (TV/Radio section)

- Tune in to our daily radio programs or listen on the Internet

- Watch our programming on TV or live on the Internet

Internet Ministry
www.gwwm.com

A Fountain
of Spiritual Wisdom

Our Servers
Serve His Purpose...
Gary Whetstone Worldwide Ministries
at www.gwwm.com

Anyplace you have access to
the web, you have access to our ministry,
24 hours a day, 7 days a week!

You can find:
- Prayer
- Biblical helps
- Live TV & Radio programs
- Resources to help answer your questions
- Online product catalog of Books & Tapes
- Descriptions of courses from the School of
  Biblical Studies
- Downloads of sample Bible school lessons
- Ministry information & help
- Dr. Gary Whetstone's itinerary

Visit our web site, or call 1 (302) 324-5400
and put Gary Whetstone Worldwide
Ministries at your fingertips.

Pastor Gary invites you to:

Victory Christian Fellowship
*One of the Fastest-Growing Churches
on the U.S. East Coast!*

SERVICE SCHEDULE

You Can Watch Live on the Internet!

Saturday Evening	7:00 p.m.	Worship & Teaching
Sunday Morning	8:30 a.m.	Worship & Teaching
	11:00 a.m.	Worship & Teaching
Sunday Evening	6:00 p.m.	Water Baptism
	7:00 p.m.	Worship & Teaching
Wednesday	7:00 p.m.	Worship & Teaching

This church is dedicated to reaching out to meet your family's needs and to help you grow strong spiritually through the revelation knowledge of God's Word. Your faith will be strengthened as you see that Word in action! Visit today or call for prayer.

VICTORY CHRISTIAN FELLOWSHIP
100 Wilton Blvd.
New Castle, DE 19720 U.S.A.
PHONE: 1 (302) 324-5400
FAX: 1 (302) 324-5448
WEB SITE: www.gwwm.com
E-MAIL: info@gwwm.com

(On Rte. 40, just past the Rte. 13/40 split at Wilton)

Gary Whetstone

Gary Whetstone is the Senior Pastor and Founder of Victory Christian Fellowship in New Castle, Delaware, and Founder of Gary Whetstone Worldwide Ministries. He holds an earned doctorate in Religious Education.

Since personally experiencing God's miraculous deliverance and healing in 1971, Dr. Whetstone has devoted his life to helping others experience freedom through God's Word. Today, he frequently ministers around the world in churches, seminars, and evangelistic crusades. Gifted in teaching, Dr. Whetstone provides practical biblical instruction wherever he ministers and has seen God work powerful signs, wonders, and miracles. Hundreds of thousands have become born-again, Spirit-filled, healed, and set free.

Having a great burden to minister to the local community, Pastor Gary Whetstone and his church have launched life-changing outreaches in several areas. These include HIV/AIDS; substance and alcohol abuse; inner-city community outreach centers; Saturday Sidewalk Sunday School; food and clothing outreach programs; and many large evangelistic campaigns, such as the dramatic production "Jesus, Light of the World," which draws over 45,000 people annually.

Desiring to spread the truth and good news of the Gospel throughout the world, Dr. Whetstone's passion is to see the Word of God cover the earth as the waters cover the seas. This vision is being accomplished through many ministry outreaches. These include sending mission and evangelism teams around the globe; radio and television broadcasting; ministry through the Internet; and the School of Biblical Studies. An extensive audio and video training program, this school equips Christians to experience God's presence and to understand the Bible. Today, this training program is established in hundreds of churches in North and South America, Australia, Europe, Asia, and Africa. In addition to local church and international branch locations, the School of Biblical Studies is available to individuals by extension in their homes using audio cassettes, videotapes, CDs, CD-ROMs, and VCDs. Currently, this home-study program is in English but soon will be available in Spanish and other languages.

Gary Whetstone has appeared on many national and international radio and television programs, and has authored key books, among which are *The Victorious Walk, How to Identify and Remove Curses!, Make Fear Bow, Millionaire Mentality,* and his personal testimony of miraculous deliverance and healing in *Conquering Your Unseen Enemies.* The large number of study guides he has produced are testaments to his gifting in practical biblical teaching and are available for use with his numerous video and audio teaching series. Many of these materials are or soon will be available not only in English, but also in Spanish, French, and other languages.

God has gifted Dr. Whetstone with an incredible business sense and ability, enabling him to publish a series of teachings from *Purchasing and Negotiations* to *Success in Business* and *Millionaire Mentality,* which has aired on his 15-year-long radio program, "Power Impact." This broadcast currently reaches an audience of over four million listeners on the East Coast of the United States.

Dr. Whetstone and his wife of nearly 30 years, Faye, have a particularly dynamic testimony of a restored marriage, which achieved national attention and was the cover story in *Charisma* magazine. Gary and Faye now conduct annual Marriage Advance seminars for couples looking to deeply enrich their relationships.

Their two adult children, Eric and Laurie, along with daughter-in-law, Rebecca, and grandson, Isaiah, are involved actively in local and international outreaches for Jesus Christ. To arrange a speaking engagement for Gary or Faye Whetstone, please contact:

Gary Whetstone Worldwide Ministries
P.O. Box 10050
Wilmington, DE 19850 U.S.A.
PHONE: 1 (302) 324-5400 • FAX: 1 (302) 324-5448
WEB SITE: www.gwwm.com • E-MAIL: info@gwwm.com

Gary Whetstone Worldwide Ministries
Product and Information Order Form

☐ Rev.   ☐ Mr.   ☐ Mrs.   ☐ Ms.   ☐ Miss   (Please print)

Name_____

Address_____

City_____ State_____ ZIP_____

Home Phone (_____) _____ Work Phone (_____) _____

E-mail_____

Please send information about the following to me:
- ☐ Ministry Products (Catalog)
- ☐ Gary Whetstone Worldwide Ministries (Information and Itinerary)
- ☐ School of Victorious Living (Audio/video teachings)
- ☐ School of Biblical Studies (Delaware campuses or out-of-state sites)
- ☐ School of Biblical Studies (Audio-correspondence program)
- ☐ School of Ministerial Training (Delaware campus)
- ☐ Victory Christian Fellowship (Church)

☐ **Pastor Gary, please pray for me. I am enclosing my prayer needs on a separate page.**

☐ **Pastor Gary, enclosed on a separate sheet is my testimony of how this book and/or your ministry ministered to me.**

Please send the following products to me:

Quantity	Item #	Title	Price	Total
			$	$
			$	$
			$	$
			$	$

(U.S.A.) SHIPPING & HANDLING Up to $10.00....$1.50 $10.01-$50.00...$3.50 $50.01-Up.........$5.00		
	Subtotal	$
	Shipping/Handling	$
	TOTAL	$

Credit Card: ☐ MasterCard   ☐ VISA   ☐ American Express   ☐ Discover

Account No._____

Expiration Date_____

Signature_____

Please make all checks payable in U.S. Dollars to "G.W.W.M."
Allow 4-6 weeks for delivery. No C.O.D.'s accepted.

Send your order and payment to:
Gary Whetstone Worldwide Ministries
P.O. Box 10050 • Wilmington, DE 19850 U.S.A.
PHONE: 1 (302) 324-5400 • FAX: 1 (302) 324-5448
WEB SITE: www.gwwm.com • E-Mail: info@gwwm.com

Notes

Notes